Guitar Sound Effects

by Jake Hertzog and Ueli Dörig

Dedicated to my incredible family,
who have always supported me.

–Jake Hertzog

For Tobias, Andrea, Lara & Leonie

–Ueli Dörig

PLAYBACK+
Speed • Pitch • Balance • Loop

To access audio visit:
www.halleonard.com/mylibrary

Enter Code
4423-4241-6369-2227

ISBN 978-1-4950-8818-6

HAL•LEONARD®

Visit Hal Leonard Online at
www.halleonard.com

Contact Us:
Hal Leonard
7777 West Bluemound Road
Milwaukee, WI 53213
Email: info@halleonard.com

In Europe contact:
Hal Leonard Europe Limited
Distribution Centre, Newmarket Road
Bury St Edmunds, Suffolk, IP33 3YB
Email: info@halleonardeurope.com

In Australia contact:
Hal Leonard Australia Pty. Ltd.
4 Lentara Court
Cheltenham, Victoria, 3192 Australia
Email: info@halleonard.com.au

Contents

Acknowledgments

Jake Hertzog

Thank you so much to Ueli Dörig, Erica Duncan, Chris Moore, University of Arkansas Music Department, The Manhattan School of Music, Berklee College of Music, and all my inspiring students and teachers.

Ueli Dörig

I'd like to thank my beautiful wife Claudia for keeping me company on my adventurous journeys, the fantastic staff at Hal Leonard for all their professional support, and last, but most certainly not least, I'd like to thank my brother-in-arms Jake Hertzog for being such a wonderful artist, educator, and friend.

Credits

These tracks were recorded and mixed by Chris Moore at East Hall Recording, Fayetteville, Arkansas and mastered by Kurt Lundvall, New York, NY. They feature Jake Hertzog on guitars.

All Photography by Erica Duncan

Introduction

This book will give you an overview of many of the most commonly used contemporary guitar effects. It is divided into five parts. In Part 1, Unplugged, we will examine sound effects and techniques that can be created with only the guitar and your hands. Part 2, Plugged, discusses effects and techniques that can be created on the guitar using equipment such as amplifiers, pedals, and recording studio technology. Parts 3 and 4 discuss some experimental techniques and, in the final section of the book, ten short etudes combine the many sound effects and techniques in musical examples to illustrate ways to use them.

Before we go into the techniques themselves, it is helpful to present the sounds of the guitar that will be the basis of all these effects.

Common Sounds

ACOUSTIC GUITARS

There are many kinds of acoustic guitars out there, and you can break them down by the types of wood used in the construction, the types of bodies, and the different kind of strings.

Nylon string guitars are most commonly used for classical music. They have resonant bodies and a very distinct sound. Though almost always played purely acoustically, there are electric nylon string guitars that were created to capture the unique nylon string sound in an amplified situation.

 a) Nylon String, b) Steel String c), Hollow Body Unplugged, d) Hollow Body Plugged

Track 1

Example 1

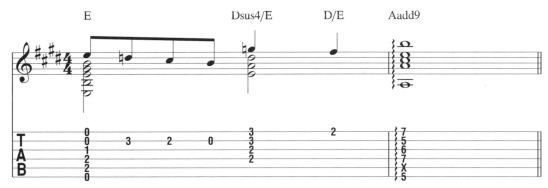

Famous Recordings of Nylon String Guitars:

* Julian Bream – "En Los Trigales"

* John Williams – Four Lute Suites of Johann Sebastian Bach

Nylon String Guitar

Steel string guitars are made from a wide variety of woods and, though often played acoustically, many have built-in pickups and electronics to use with amplifiers or other audio systems. Most of the plugged effects in this book will work on steel string acoustic guitars.

Famous Recordings of Steel String Guitars:
- Leo Kottke – "Morning Is the Long Way Home"
- Al Di Meola, John McLaughlin, Paco de Lucia – "Mediterranean Sundance/Rio Ancho" (Live)

Steel String Guitar

Hollow body guitars are usually intended to be used with amplifiers and often include some type of pickup system. These guitars are commonly associated with jazz and blues music. For a very unique sound, experiment with flat wound strings.

Famous Recordings of Hollow Body Guitars:
- Joe Pass – "Stella by Starlight"
- Wes Montgomery – "D Natural Blues"

Hollow Body Guitar

ELECTRIC GUITARS

Electric guitars have three distinct varieties in their construction. **Solid body** guitars refer to one continuous block of wood used on the body, and **semi-hollow body** guitars have a carved open chamber in a solid block of wood. Semi-hollow instruments often have small holes in the body, like a violin. Additionally, **chambered body** guitars have open carvings in the wood that are covered. All electric guitars share one important feature, and that is the way that sound is "picked-up" from the strings. Pickups are magnets that electrify a guitar. There are several types:

Single coil pickups use one magnetic coil and have a very distinct sound. Classic guitars such as the Fender Stratocaster make use of these pickups. They are susceptible to electric hum, which is the reason that other single-coil variations, such as the "noiseless" single coil pickups, were subsequently invented and commonly used. On Track 2, the five different pickup configurations on a Stratocaster-type guitar are demonstrated with an open E chord before Examples 1 and 2 (see next page) are played.

Track 2

5-Way Pickup Selection on Fender Stratocaster
(neck, neck/middle, middle, middle/bridge, bridge)

Example 2

Single Coil Pickups

Humbucking Pickups

Humbucker pickups (pictured above) are made with two magnetic coils operating opposite each other so that the "hum" of the single coil is canceled. They tend to run more powerfully than single coils, which is why many heavily distorted sounds demand humbucker pickups. Classic guitars such as the Gibson Les Paul feature humbucker pickups. On Track 3, the three different pickup configurations on a Les Paul-type guitar are demonstrated with an open E chord before Examples 1 and 2 are played.

Track 3

3-Way Pickup Selection on Humbucker Pickups (neck, middle, bridge)

Piezo pickups are small pickups inside the bridge of a guitar (acoustic or electric) designed to give an organic and slightly acoustic sound. Many different types of guitars include piezo pickups for extra color variations.

Pickup blends are a common feature of most electric guitars and acoustic guitars as well. Switches on the instruments allow for multiple pickups to be activated simultaneously. This means that the pickup near the neck and the pickup near the bridge or middle position will both be activated and thus produce a sound that is different from the sound of either one by itself. Some guitars even include a knob to blend the volumes of these multiple sound sources. Blending a magnetic pickup with a piezo is also a commonly used sound. A **coil-tap** is a switch that turns a humbucker into a single coil pickup by turning off one of the coils.

SPECIAL GUITARS

Fretless guitars produce a wonderfully unique sound, due to the lack of frets. They are very well suited to playing non-western music as the intonation can be determined by the player. Although it can be difficult to play full chords in tune on a fretless guitar, three-note voicings are usually playable.

Famous Fretless Guitarists:
- Dave Fiuczynski
- Ron Thal (Bumblefoot)

Resonators have a metal section of the body and produce a unique resonant sound. They have a bowl shape, an enlarged sound hole, and most often have steel strings. These guitars are great for slide and open tunings but can be well suited to many types of music due to their distinctive tone. Track 4 features examples 1 and 2 played on a resonator guitar. Note that Example 2 is fingered slightly differently in order to accentuate the qualities of the resonator's tonal character.

Resonator Guitar

 Resonator Guitar

Track 4

Famous Resonator Guitarists:
- Josh Graves
- Taj Mahal

Synth guitars can refer to any guitar with a MIDI controller or electronic interface. Through the use of electronics, the guitar can be used as a controller to activate any sound in the player's software. Most synth guitars have magnetic pickups as well and wiring that allows the player to blend the volumes of the guitar's magnetic pickups with the volume of the MIDI sounds. Many hybrid timbres can be created in this way. A guitar equipped with MIDI technology can be set to sound like any virtual instrument, such as a piano or a full orchestra.

Today, there are two main types of guitar-synthesizers:

- **Guitar-synth using guitars**: These are regular electric guitars equipped with special electronic sensors that actuate a synthesizer.
- **Guitar-synth using non-guitar controllers**: These are specifically designed guitar-like MIDI controllers.

Famous Recordings of Synth Guitars:
- Pat Metheny – "Question and Answer" (Live)
- The Police – "Don't Stand So Close to Me"

AMPLIFIERS

There are three main categories of amplifiers: **tube**, **solid state**, and **digital** (modeling).

Tube amplifiers use vacuum tubes to increase the power of an input signal. This has always given them a distinct and iconic sound. Pushing more power through the tubes will get you that classic warm and crunchy sound. Track 5 demonstrates Examples 1 and 2 played through a tube amp.

 Tube Amplifier

Track 5

Famous Recordings of Tube Amplifiers:
- Eric Clapton – "Layla"
- Jeff Beck – "Cause We've Ended as Lovers"

Solid-state amplifiers do not have tubes so they use regular electrical components, such as transistors and diodes, to amplify the input signal. They have a very different sound than a tube amp, and solid-state distortion can get much more powerful wave clipping than a tube overdrive. These amps also have an instantly recognizable sound. Track 6 demonstrates Examples 1 and 2 played through a solid-state amp.

 Solid-State Amplifier

Track 6

Famous Recordings of Solid-State Amplifiers:
- The Police – "Every Breath You Take"
- Creedence Clearwater Revival – "I Heard It Through the Grapevine"

Digital amplifier modeling is the use of a computer to simulate the sound of a traditional tube or solid-state amp. Amp modeling can be built into an actual guitar amp or come in the form of a pedal, rack unit, or software plugin. The advantage of amp modeling is the endless variation and control over a tone and the ability to simulate many components at the same time. The disadvantage is that people who spend a lot of time listening find the digital sound less desirable than the warmer sound of analog gear. It is certainly worth experimenting with amp modeling however, as the increases in computing power continue to provide us with better and better-sounding amp software.

Common Right-Hand Techniques

The way a player uses the right hand, or picking hand, to strike the strings has a large influence on the basic tone. Because of this, it is important to review the most common right-hand techniques.

A **plectrum** or **pick** is any object used to strike the strings. Most guitar picks are made of plastic, wood, metal, or other materials such as shell or bone. The material and thickness of the pick greatly affect the tone, and experimenting with many different picks will give you a wide range of sounds, from dark to bright and harsh to delicate. The plectrum can be held between the thumb and index finger or attached to the thumb (called a **thumb pick**). Track 7 demonstrates the same phrase played with three different right-hand techniques.

Different Picks

Thumb Pick

 a) Played with Pick, b) Played Fingerstyle, c) Played Hybrid Style (pick and fingers)

Track 7

Example 3

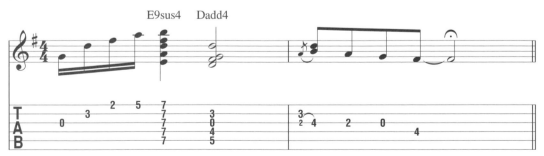

Listen to Track 8 to hear the same phrase played with various picks.

Different Pick Types: a) Very Light, b) Light, c) Medium, d) Heavy, e) Thumb Pick, f) Felt Pick

Example 4

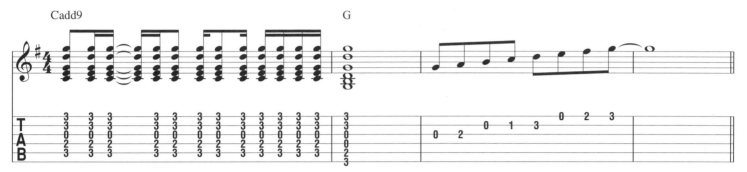

Fingerstyle (or classical style) uses only the fingers of the striking hand, and the nails or flesh of the fingers produce the tone. Playing in this way allows the guitarist greater freedom in striking multiple strings simultaneously. The most common method is to play using the thumb and the first three fingers of the hand, though some players utilize the fourth finger as well. Placement of the hand and quality of the nails are important to getting a great sound, so be mindful and experiment to find the most comfortable way to play. Some players use synthetic nails for a more powerful sound than natural nails can provide.

Hybrid picking makes use of the pick and two or three of the remaining fingers. The advantage is that it allows some fingerstyle techniques to be used while holding a pick. However, it prohibits use of the thumb and first finger for proper fingerstyle playing.

Some iconic musicians, such as Wes Montgomery and Jeff Beck, have very personal and unusual picking techniques. Every player should experiment with many combinations of techniques until they find the one (or ones) most suitable for their own style. However, one should first and foremost consider the three most common and efficient techniques described above.

Tonal variations can easily be produced by moving the picking hand along the plane of the string—towards the neck for a darker sound, and towards the bridge for a brighter sound. This holds true regardless of picking style. This is often notated in written guitar music with the terms **sul tasto** (toward the neck) and **ponticello** (toward the bridge). Track 9 demonstrates this with single notes and chords.

Sul Tasto to Ponticello, Single Notes and Chord

Left-handed guitarists should have no trouble adapting these techniques with the left hand instead of the right, although you should make sure your guitar is properly set up for left-handed playing.

How to Use This Book

There are two main sections in this book. In the Unplugged section, you will learn about physical techniques and alterations to the instrument. The Plugged section focuses on technology and applications used to generate sounds from the instrument. Because the scope of guitar sounds and techniques is vast, this book is intended to be a guide for standard techniques, as well as extended techniques and sonic concepts. We hope that guitarists and composers of all levels will be able to use this book as an encyclopedia—an insight into the full palette of sounds the guitar is capable of creating.

About the Audio

To access the audio tracks for download or streaming, visit **www.halleonard.com/mylibrary** and enter the code found on page 1 of this book. The examples with accompanying audio tracks are marked with audio icons throughout the book.

How to Use Extended Techniques

Practicing extended techniques (and standard ones) will help you enhance your knowledge of your instrument. Understanding the guitar better allows you to have ultimate control over your sound and your music. Experimentation is key in finding a personal and musical approach to using all the various techniques discussed in this book. Always remember: it is one thing to be capable of playing an extended technique or dialing up a sound; it's another to use it musically.

A Note for Composers

Musicians who are not primarily guitarists will find this book a useful and practical tour through the sonic language of modern guitarists. The guitar has tremendous potential beyond its humble origins as an accompaniment instrument, and this guide will assist you in finding ways to communicate with your guitarist collaborators, as well as open more possibilities for your use of the guitar.

Part I: Unplugged Effects
Chapter 1: Pitch

1.1. Harmonics

Harmonics are a beautiful bell-like effect that can be played on any pitch that the guitar can make. The concept of harmonics is based on the **overtone series**. When a string vibrates, it produces a sound called the **fundamental**. This is the primary pitch that we hear. Inside this pitch, however, are many higher frequencies called **harmonics**. They vibrate according to the overtone series at mathematical multiples of the fundamental. What this means is if you are able to strike a string and then instantly prevent a portion of that string from vibrating, you will isolate a harmonic and achieve a different pitch than the fundamental.

There are two common ways of playing harmonics on the guitar: natural harmonics and false harmonics.

Natural harmonics are created by playing one of the open strings and placing your finger gently on the string above the desired fret (note: touch the string but do not push down). Because some frequencies in the overtones are more powerful than others, these natural harmonics only occur at specific frets. At each of these frets, you will hear a harmonic that is an interval above the fundamental pitch (in this case, the open string).

Strike the low E string, then place your finger on the string above the 12th fret. You will hear an E note one octave higher than the open string. Now run your finger gently along the string toward the headstock while continuing to strike the string, and you will discover the following harmonics:

 Harmonics on the Low E String: a) Clean, b) With Distortion

Track 10

12th Fret	E	One Octave higher
9th Fret (or 4th Fret)	G♯	2 Octaves + Major 3rd
7th Fret	B	One Octave + Perfect 5th
5th Fret	E	Two Octaves
3rd Fret	B	Two Octaves + Perfect 5th
2nd Fret	G♯	Three Octaves + Major 3rd*

*This one is difficult. Try it with new strings and distortion!

Other natural harmonics are possible, but they will be more difficult to sound. However, feel free to experiment. When you apply heavy distortion to an electric guitar (that by definition boosts the overtones), you will have an easier time sounding natural harmonics.

These harmonics will repeat above the 12th fret, as well. Depending on your instrument, pickups, and strings, you may get a clearer sound above or below the 12th fret. These intervals will be identical for the natural harmonics on the other five strings as well. Try to put together short melodies using only the natural harmonics!

Example 5

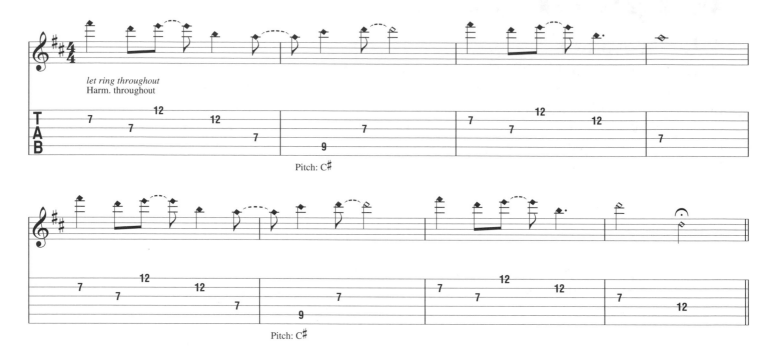

let ring throughout
Harm. throughout

Pitch: C♯

Pitch: C♯

Famous Recordings Featuring Harmonics:
- Leo Kottke – "Little Martha"
- Van Halen – "Panama"

False harmonics (also called **artificial harmonics**) are slightly more difficult to play, but they allow you to create a harmonic on any pitch. Grip the pick so that the tip is barely over the edge of your fingers. Then fret any note and dig in with your right hand so that, as you strike the string, the flesh of your finger instantly strikes the string after the pick. This may take some practice, but it will give you a sharp, high harmonic based on any fretted note. This technique also works very well on an electric guitar with heavy distortion. This type of false harmonic is also commonly called a **pinch harmonic**.

 False Harmonics: a) Clean, b) Distortion

Track 12

Another fantastic harmonic technique is to take advantage of the clarity and tone of the natural harmonics on any note by striking a harmonic 12 frets above a fretted note. For example, you can play a B♭ on the G string at the third fret and then play a false harmonic on the 15th fret by touching the harmonic with your index finger and holding the pick with the thumb and middle finger. Using this technique, you can play melodies by "following" your fretting hand with your picking hand. You can also play full chords in harmonics by striking many notes in rapid succession or gently using your palm to rest 12 frets above any chord and strumming lightly. This is very difficult but worth the practice as it is a beautiful effect.

The **harp harmonic effect** is a spectacular technique that involves alternating between a harmonic (natural or false) and a fretted note. It works by first arranging your fretting hand into a chord. You then play the harmonic 12 frets above one note in the chord. Immediately following that note, strike a lower-pitched string without the harmonic. Continue this harmonic/natural pattern to create a gorgeous harp-like palette on a chord or chord sequence.

 Harp Harmonic Effect – Chord and Arpeggio

Track 13

1.2. Bends

Bent notes are one of the most evocative sounds a guitar can create. Because every player has different muscles and hands, the sound of bent notes is intensely personal and often helps define a given player's style.

The way to bend strings on the guitar is to use the strength of the wrist and the palm of the hand to push strings upwards or pull them downwards. The top three (thinner) strings are generally pushed up toward the ceiling, while the lower three strings are usually pulled down toward the floor. Depending on the strength of each of your fingers, you might find it helpful to use more than one finger for a deep bend. Do this by "stacking" the fingers behind each other for extra strength.

Mastering bends and incorporating them in your playing by gaining control takes practice, but the most challenging aspect of bending is intonation. To practice bending in tune, you need to feel how high the bend needs to be to get the desired pitch.

Play an E note, for example. Then play one half step above that note, F. Now fret the E note and bend it up to match the pitch of the F note you just played. Do this a few times. Next, repeat this exercise using an F♯ instead of the F. In other words, bend the E up a whole step to match the pitch of F♯. Play the E again and try to bend up a minor 3rd to G. Keep repeating until you can easily hit the target pitches. The farther the bend, the more you'll need to use additional strength coming from the elbow and the shoulder. If you can, try bending the E up to a G♯ (major 3rd)!

 Bending Practice

Track 14

Example 6

As bending becomes more and more effortless for you, try all combinations of strings on different areas of the neck (bending is easiest in the middle of the neck). Try bending two or even three strings at the same time. Take a simple melody and replace as many notes with bends as you can. There are many exciting ways to utilize bent notes in your playing. Keep experimenting!

A **neck bend** is one in which you grab the headstock of the guitar and pull back on it or push it forward, thereby extending or contracting the string. This produces a unique-sounding bend, much like a whammy bar effect.

 Neck Bend

Track 15

> Famous Recordings Featuring Bends:
> - Stevie Ray Vaughan & Double Trouble – "Texas Flood"
> - Albert King – "I'll Play the Blues For You"

1.3. Vibrato

Almost every instrument attempts to mimic the human voice, and developing a rich **vibrato** technique on the guitar is very useful in this regard. There are many varieties of vibrato techniques and, just like bending, they can be very personal and defining qualities of a player's sound. However, there are three main movements you can practice to get that great "singing" quality.

Begin with a note in the middle of the neck (just as with bending, the middle of the neck is the easiest place to practice vibrato). We'll use the A note at fret 10 on the B string. As you rock the finger toward the bridge and then back toward the headstock, the pitch will waver. This is sometimes called **lateral vibrato**. The second technique is to do a miniature bend by rocking the finger back and forth across the neck—enough to waver the pitch but not enough to bend up to a half step. This is sometimes called **vertical vibrato**. A third variation is to combine the two into a **circular vibrato**. Experiment with the arm, elbow, wrist, and shoulder to get variety in how the pitch wavers.

Depth refers to how much the vibrato pitch varies from the original note. **Rate** is determined by how fast the pitch wobbles back and forth between the two extremes. To get the most out of vibrato and to develop the greatest control, it's important to practice exercises that vary the depth and rate.

 Vibrato Drills A–H

Track 16

> A) Start with a very slow, medium depth vibrato, then increase the rate gradually to as fast as you can.
>
> B) Start with a very fast vibrato and gradually decrease the rate.
>
> C) Start with a very deep vibrato and slowly make it shallower.
>
> D) Start with a shallow vibrato and increase the depth.
>
> E) Listen to some opera singers and try to imitate the way they use vibrato in their voices.
>
> F) Listen to some violin or cello recordings and then imitate the vibrato you hear.
>
> G) Listen to some blues guitarists and jazz horn players and try to match those types of vibrato.
>
> H) Set a slow metronome and vary the rate of your vibrato while keeping the same tempo using eighth notes, triplets, and 16th notes.

These are just a few of the many ways you can practice vibrato to incorporate greater control of it in your playing. The more you work on these exercises, the more they will be incorporated naturally in your sound!

Note: Musical style is an important consideration here. Some styles, such as blues, require more vibrato, and others, such as bebop, require less.

Famous Guitarists with Beautiful Vibratos:
- Andrés Segovia
- Eric Clapton

1.4. Whammy Bar

The **whammy bar** on the electric guitar can make some extremely unique sounds. This has become a signature sound for certain genres, such as surf guitar and heavy metal. Though most commonly found on Fender guitars, a whammy bar can be added to almost any electric guitar on the market.

Because the bar has more room to give on the "push" side than on the "pull" side, the most basic technique is to bend a note down by striking a note, pushing the bar down, and releasing it, allowing the note to come back up. You can bend very far this way! The bar also can be used to bend upward by striking the note and then pulling the bar up and releasing it back down. Try this technique with a single note as well as full chords for some exciting possibilities.

Try playing a **dive** by striking a lower note or chord (with distortion if possible) and pushing the bar down as far as it can go. Then bring it slowly back up. Another great technique is to hold the bar in your picking hand while playing melodies and, by applying slight pressure to the whammy bar, you will be adding gentle bends to various notes in the line, making the entire phrase sound very "slippery."

Depending on the type of guitar you are playing, striking the strings behind the nut will give you a very high pitch sound that you can then bend using the whammy bar. This is a fantastic effect with distortion. **Fluttering** the whammy bar very quickly up and down is also a great textural effect to use on single notes or chords.

A final whammy bar trick is to use it on a melody line. Play a phrase and, on the final note, push or pull the whammy bar, and it should give you a great bend and extra sustain.

To develop even greater control of the whammy bar, practice bending to exact pitches—the same way you would practice bending fretted notes (see Example 6). For example, practice bending the low E string down to D or C♯. Next, play a fretted note and pull up a whole step. These kinds of exercises extend your whammy abilities greatly!

 Whammy Bar: a) Chord, b) Dive, c) Melody

Track 17

Famous Recordings Featuring the Whammy Bar:
- Jimi Hendrix – "Star Spangled Banner"
- Chet Atkins – "Mister Sandman"

1.5. Slide Guitar

Using a **slide** on the guitar will give you a whole new range of sonic textures to work with that cannot be made using the fingers alone. Along with the tonal possibilities, slide guitar can be used to tap into a unique melodic and phrasing language as many slide guitar masters have demonstrated. Almost anything can be used as a slide, but the most common slides are made from glass, metal, or plastic. They all have different tonal qualities, so it is best to experiment with several different types. The slide can be placed on any finger, but few players place it on their index finger. If the slide is placed on the middle finger, the stronger first and third fingers are available for lines and bends. Many players wear the slide on the third or fourth fingers to achieve greater control. Try each finger to find the most comfortable and natural position.

The major challenge with slide guitar is the intonation. Place the slide gently on the high E string. Do not apply any pressure, but rest the slide directly above a fret wire. Strike the string to play the note. Now compare this pitch to the normally fretted note to check your intonation. Repeat the process until the two pitches are indistinguishable. If you move slightly above or below a fret with the slide you will get a pitch in between two notes. This opens up many possibilities of playing slide guitar using different intonation systems, and it also allows for some spectacular bending and phrasing effects. For example, to create vibrato with a slide, play the note and then move the slide back and forth above and below the fret in equal distances.

Slide Placement

As you get more comfortable, play through some scales using all six strings. Try sliding between each note and then moving distinctly from note to note without the slide effect (but while still using the slide). Try playing scales on only one string for a very slippery sound. Try to use the slide on two or three strings at a time. You can try to imitate the sound of a pedal steel guitar by sliding chords around. Alternate and open tunings are very commonly used with the slide, as it makes chordal playing easier.

 A Minor Scale with Slide

Track 18

Famous Slide Players:
- Duane Allman
- Derek Trucks
- Sonny Landreth

Note: While playing slide, it is helpful to raise the action of the guitar strings. Higher action will give you clearer tone and greater playability when using the slide. Because of this, it's not uncommon for players to set up a guitar for exclusive (or at least predominant) slide use.

Chapter 2: Rhythm

2.1. Tremolo

Tremolo is a texture created by attacking a note or chord repeatedly as fast as possible without regard to tempo or beat. There are two common ways to create this effect using different right-hand styles.

If you are using a pick, alternate the pick back and forth across any open string. Gradually increase the speed until you can no longer clearly hear individual attacks. That is the tremolo effect. Everyone has a natural limitation on how fast they can play like this and certainly for how long, so do not focus on reaching an absolute speed. Simply play as fast and relaxed as you are able.

If you are playing fingerstyle, then you can alternate two or three (or even four!) fingers striking a string in rapid succession. Once again, increase the speed as much as you can. Now you have the tremolo sound.

Try playing melodies on one string while using the tremolo effect; then try playing lines across several strings. Next, try playing double stops and full chords as a tremolo effect. For this, you might find it helpful to use the thumb or a very soft pick to get a fluid multi-note tremolo.

 F Lydian Scale with Tremolo

Track 19

Example 7

Famous Recordings Featuring Tremolo:

- Pepe Romero – *Recuerdos De La Alhambra*
- David Russell – *Una Limosna Por El Amor De Dios*
- Van Halen – "Eruption"

Health Warning: Do not practice tremolo techniques for long periods of time and ensure you are using proper and relaxed technique. It is very strenuous on the muscles, and if they do not get a chance to rest following rigorous activity, you risk a repetitive strain injury.

2.2. Sweep Picking and Economy Picking

Sweep picking and **economy picking** are phenomenal techniques that drastically increase the speed at which you can play notes while using a pick. It takes some practice, but the basic principle is to keep the pick moving in the same direction if possible when you switch to an adjacent string.

Imagine economy picking as strumming in miniature. Let us look at an A minor scale, using three notes per string and beginning on the E string. We will use five of the strings to get a full two-octave scale. We can see that there are four places where sweeping increases speed and economy of motion; this is every time we transition to the next string.

Play the scale again, only this time, whenever you move to the following string, play one continuous downstroke through both strings. Then go backwards and use one continuous upstroke each time you switch strings. This is sweep picking in a nutshell.

 Sweep Picking of A Minor Scale: a) Slow, b) Faster,
c) Sweep/Economy Picking Improvisation

Track 20

Example 8

Note: Whereas **economy picking** generally applies to scalar playing, **sweep picking** generally applies to arpeggios, in which you're moving through several strings at a time. Some guitarists use these terms interchangeably, but it is helpful when practicing to work on them as separate but related skills.

Tip: A **rest stroke** is performed when your pick comes to rest on the next string after plucking or picking. It is helpful, when economy picking certain passages, to include a rest stroke in the right-hand pattern.

Economy picking works best when there is an odd number of notes per string, as it provides a shortcut to getting to that next note on the following string. Three-note-per-string patterns work very well with this technique. To get other patterns to work well, try using legato technique in the left hand so that, no matter how many notes are on each string, you only need to attack any given string one or three times.

For example, you could play a two-note-per-string scale, such as a pentatonic scale, by picking the first note on each string and hammering to (or pulling off to) the second note. This gives your pick time to sweep past the first string and prepare to attack the second string in the sequence. This is a perfect example of how to include the rest stroke in sweep picking.

Sweeping patterns or arpeggios using a one-note-per-string approach are also a strikingly awesome effect. Try playing a Dm7 arpeggio with this technique:

Example 9

Play it forward and backward using a downstroke sweep followed by an upstroke sweep. Experiment with different combinations of legato and sweep picking to find as many patterns as you can. As you get comfortable with sweeping, it will get easier and easier to combine the technique with alternate picking.

Tip: In almost any melodic passage, there might be places where a short burst of sweep picking will make that passage sound smoother and allow you to play it faster. Whatever the pattern, always look for the sweep shortcuts to make it smooth and fast. Keep in mind, however, that sweep picking can often sacrifice the clarity of the notes in favor of speed.

A **rake** is a mini-sweep covering only a few strings, and the principle is the same. But sometimes with raking, the idea is to hit the strings so quickly that the effect is more percussive than harmonic. It's more like a very strong accent. Triplets work very well as a raked figure. Track 21 demonstrates the Dm7 sweep arpeggio from Example 9 and a quick rake figure (Example 10).

 a) Sweep: Slow and Fast, b) Rake

Track 21

Example 10

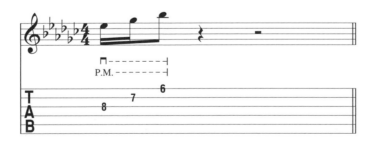

One note per string also works great. A rake can also be a great effect if you slightly palm mute with the right hand to accentuate the percussiveness of the attack. Dig in hard to get a really great raking sound. For example, if we play a minor triad arpeggio on the top three strings and apply a palm mute, we will get a very quick, quasi-wood, block-type roll of notes.

Famous Sweep Picking Guitarists:
- Yngwie Malmsteen
- Frank Gambale

2.3. Palm Muting

Palm muting is a very common effect that allows the guitar to have a wider range of percussive and tonal qualities. To create the palm mute, place the side of the picking hand very gently on top of the bridge of the guitar. As you play a few notes, slide the picking hand slowly toward the neck and listen as the sound of the strings deaden and become more muted. As you approach the neck, the pitch of the notes will disappear, and you will hear only a percussive sound.

The ideal palm mute is created with your picking hand very close to the bridge. You can control the sound further by increasing or decreasing the pressure of the picking hand. Try this technique with distortion to get the classic heavy rock sound. Try it as part of a melody, applying and lifting the palm mute for great variation in the sound of the line.

 a) Palm Muting Technique on Open Strings, b) Use of Palm Mutes in Melody

Track 22

Famous Recordings Featuring Palm Mutes:
- Green Day – "Basket Case"
- Metallica – "Enter Sandman"

2.4. Strumming and Muted Strumming

Strumming is the most common guitar technique, but it deserves a mention here. You can strum with either the pick, fingers, or thumb; all have different tonal qualities. If you are playing with a pick, experiment with picks of varying materials and thicknesses. To practice strumming, use a metronome at a slow speed and work on getting a smooth flow of upstrokes and downstrokes.

Muted strumming is created by allowing the fingers on the left hand to rest gently on the strings without pushing them down, creating a percussive attack in lieu of notes. Try to play a chord and lift up the hand (releasing pressure) to get a muted attack; then place the chord back down for a rapid "one-two" punch. Alternating between fretted chords and muted strokes gives a great textural effect when incorporated into regular strumming patterns. It's a staple of funk guitar.

 a) Strumming at Increasing Tempos, b) Strumming with Mutes

Track 23

Tip: Experiment with strumming close to the bridge for a brighter sound (ponticello) and close to the neck (tasto) for a much darker, warmer sound.

Chapter 3: Harmonic

3.1. Open Strings

The open strings of the guitar create very special resonances on their respective notes that give the guitar its unique and luscious sound. There are many ways to use open strings for special effects that take advantage of their unique timbral quality.

Standard guitar tuning (EADGBE) has many transposable voicings. We can get a great resonant sound if we allow one or more of the notes in any given chord to be an open string instead of a fretted note.

Let's look at a Cmaj7 as an example. The open B string serves as the major 7th of the chord, and the open G string is the 5th. Now, if we move the fretted portion of this chord up two frets while leaving those open strings open, we'll get a Gmaj7 (second inversion) with the open G string as the root and the B string as the 3rd:

 Cmaj7 and Gmaj7 with Open B and G Strings

Track 24

Example 11

Almost an infinite number of fantastic and unique chord voicings can be created by using this open-string transposing technique. Here are some more examples of the original chord and a transposed version, in which the open strings become different notes:

 Transposing Open-String Shapes

Track 25

Example 12

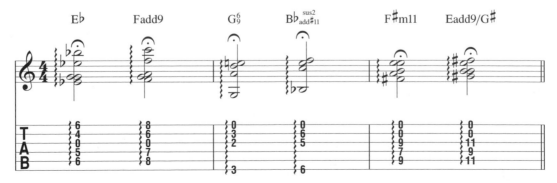

Some chords utilizing open strings are only possible in one position with one fingering. There are so many options that it is a good idea to experiment and organize your experiments based on how many open strings you are using for each chord. We can call these "non-transposable chords."

 Non-Transposable Chords

Track 26

Example 13

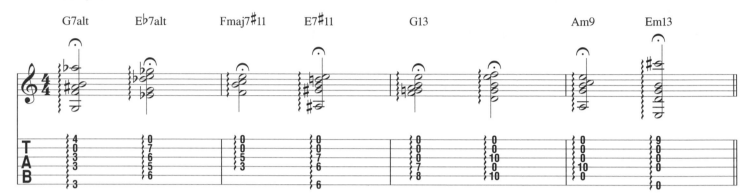

Another effective technique to expand your open-string thinking is to imagine one open string—for example, the high E string—as every possible note in a chord, and form the rest of the voicing around that note. For extra variation, you can change the quality and extensions of all these chords as well.

 Constant Open-String Chromatic Chords

Track 27

Example 14

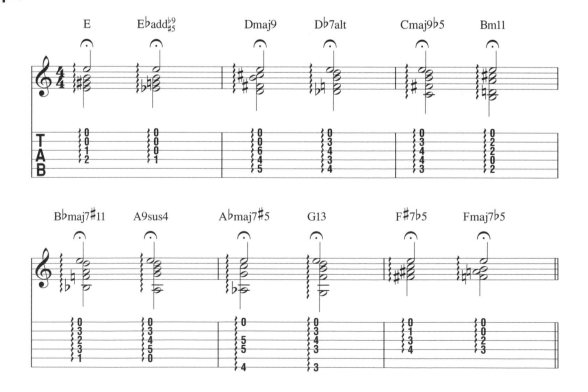

It becomes a fun game to look for as many clever uses of open strings as possible. The lower three strings can work very well as deep pedal points to take advantage of the harmonic capabilities of the guitar. Try letting the low E or A string ring out while moving fretted chords up and down the neck.

 Low Pedal Point with Fretted Chords on Top

Track 28

Example 15

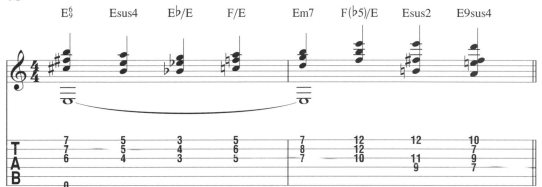

3.2. Capos

There are many kinds of capos, but they all serve the same function. Imagine moving the nut of the guitar neck up so that all the open strings retain their intervallic relationship to each other but all begin on higher pitches. For example, if you place the capo on the third fret, the open strings become G–C–F–B♭–D–G.

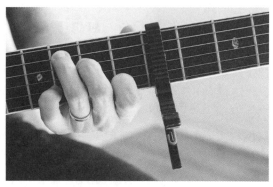

Capo Placement

 a) No Capo, b) Capo on Third Fret,
c) Transposed Open Chords with Capo on
Third Then Fifth Fret

Track 29

Note: Do not place the capo on top of the fret, but rather just behind the fret where you would normally place your finger. Try to place the capo perpendicular to the body of the guitar, parallel to the frets. If the capo is not parallel to the frets, you will experience intonation problems.

Capos open up all sorts of transposition possibilities, as they allow you to take a resonant open-string voicing and transpose it to a new key without changing the structure of the voicing. The higher you capo, the more mandolin-like your sound becomes. Capoing on the 12th fret, for example, will give a great mandolin- or balalaika-type effect.

 Mandolin/Balalaika Effect

Track 30

Example 16

*Capoed fret is "0" in tab.

You can also experiment with using a partial capo on only a few strings of the guitar for a drone effect.

 Drone String Effect

Track 31

Example 17

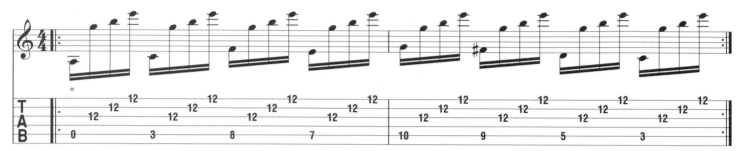

*Partial capo on strings 1-3 at 12th fret. Notes at fret 12 in tab are played as capoed open strings.

3.3. Alternate Tunings

One of the most exciting aspects of the guitar is that its tuning is not fixed. Experimenting with alternate tunings is truly a realm of endless possibility. In the alternate tuning universe, we find several commonly used alternate tunings and also an endless supply of custom tunings.

The most compelling reason to use an alternate tuning is to allow specific chords or voicings to take advantage of open-string combinations that are not found in standard tuning. This gives the instrument more resonance and a more unique sound for any particular song.

One of the most common alternate tunings is drop D tuning. This involves simply tuning the low E string down a whole step to D. This creates a surprising amount of new harmonic possibilities with lower voiced chords.

Another commonly used tuning is DADGAD, in which the strings are tuned, low to high, D–A–D–G–A–D. This is an extremely resonant tuning and is used a lot in Celtic folk music. Led Zeppelin's "Kashmir" famously uses this tuning.

Tip: You can also try a variation of this tuning using an F♯ or F instead of G to get a completely open-string major or minor chord. These types of tunings also work great with slide guitar because they allow more parallel sliding chord possibilities than in standard tuning.

Tunings get more interesting the more exotic you allow yourself to think. One fascinating example is to tune the guitar completely in 4ths (E–A–D–G–C–F) or in 5ths (E–B–F♯–C♯–G♯–D♯), like a violin.

Tip: Once you get more into experimenting with tunings, you may want to use custom string sets and many different gauges to find the best type of string combination for a special alternate tuning. You can even remove strings completely for a five-string guitar idea with a unique tuning concept.

Alternate tunings are a never-ending frontier of guitar exploration; the more you dive in, the more intriguing ideas you will find! Track 32 demonstrates the open strings played in five different tunings.

 a) Standard Tuning, b) DADGAD, c) DADF♯AD (Open D Tuning), d) EADGCF,
e) DAEBF♯ (Five-String Tuning)

Track 32

Chapter 4: Percussive

4.1. Tapping

Tapping on the guitar is a spectacular technique that greatly expands the texture and sound of the instrument. In its simplest form, tapping involves using any part of the strumming hand to hit the neck of the guitar to create a pitched sound. It will sound almost like a hammer-on with the fretting hand, but with an extra amount of slap.

Exercises

1. Depending on if you are playing with a pick or not, try tapping a few notes using the index, middle, or ring fingers on the strumming hand. Try tapping out a short melody. The notes will blend together well if you hammer on many of the left-hand pitches.

a) Tapping Between Frets, b) Tapping a Short Melody

Track 33

Example 18

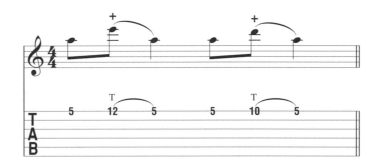

Example 19

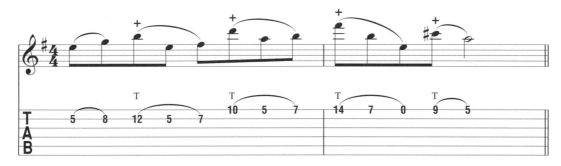

2. You can also try tapping with two or three fingers to get multiple notes (polyphony).

Tapping with Three Fingers (Polyphonic Tapping)

Track 34

Example 20

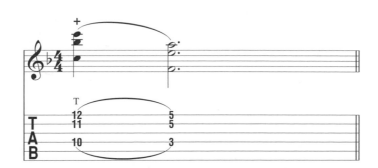

3. Next, try tapping one note and sliding the tapping finger to a second note. Then try tapping a note and releasing it forcefully enough to let the string ring (like a pull-off). If you place a fretted note behind your tapping hand, you'll hear *that* note when the tap is released.

4. Finally, try a double tap—two taps on the same note in rapid succession.

 a) Sliding Tapping Finger to a Second Note, b) Double Tap

Track 35

Example 21

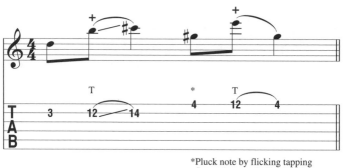

*Pluck note by flicking tapping
finger down and off string 2.

Example 22

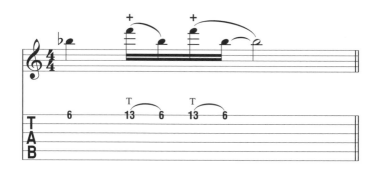

Tips: There are many great ways to incorporate tapping into your playing. For example:

- Try making tapped notes a portion of a melody or all of a melody.
- Tap a few notes at the end of a phrase or tap out a two- or three-note chord in between melodic lines.
- You can also try tapping with two hands. Do this by tapping with the fingers of the fretting hand and the picking hand. This is a great way to get interesting chords, wide intervals, and very percussive rhythms.
- To bring out the sound of tapping, try it with distortion or delay to increase the sustain of the sound and to amplify the rhythmic effect.

 a) Tapping with Two Hands, b) Same Melody with Distortion

Track 36

Example 23

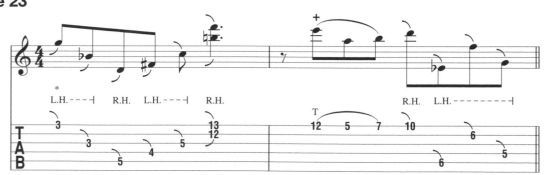

*All notes tapped or hammered/pulled.

4.2. Pick Slides

The **pick slide** is a percussive effect with a wide range of possibilities. To produce the pick slide, use one of the lower three (wound) strings on the guitar. Drag the edge of the pick down the string starting at the bridge and moving toward the neck of the guitar, applying pressure. You'll hear a grating sound; this is the pick slide. The effect is most commonly used with a good amount of distortion.

 Pick Slide: a) Clean Tone, b) Distorted Tone

Track 37

Example 24

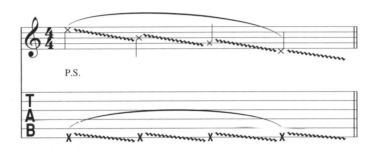

If you move the pick slowly, it will sound different than moving the pick quickly. Experiment with the speed of the pick slide and how far down the string you go. You'll also notice that the D, A, and E strings all sound slightly different with the pick slide.

Tips:

- Try this technique with distortion for a much harder, heavier, and more mechanical sound.
- You can make a distorted guitar sound like a motorcycle or muscle car by sliding up and down on the lowest three strings for that gear-shifting engine sound. Drop D tuning works great with this effect!

 Gear-Shifting Engine Sound

Track 38

4.3. String Percussion

String percussion involves muting the strings gently enough to get a pitched sound while plucking them. Depending on which string you are using and where your hand is on the string, you can get a lot of variation in the tonal quality of your sound.

 String Percussion

Track 39

Example 25

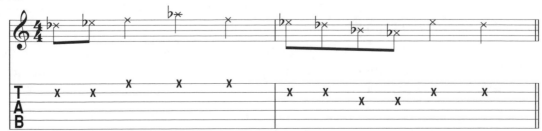

Exercises

1. Try gently resting your finger on the G string around the ninth fret. Dig in hard with the pick or your nails and get a pitched tone. Experiment with the pressure of the left hand to get the right tone. Then move your hand along the length of the string, as you would a slide, but without pushing the string down. Try alternating different strings for different sounds. If you go very far up the length of the string (above where the neck meets the body), you can achieve a great marimba-like tone.

2. Try different strumming and fingerpicking techniques to get some great percussive textures.

3. Experiment using one or multiple delay effects.

Tip: If you are playing on an electric guitar, try adding lots of reverb to enhance the effect.

4.4. The Guitar as a Drum Set

To get even more percussive sounds from a guitar, we can conceive of the instrument as if it were a drum set. The drum set has low sounds, such as the bass drum and toms, and high sounds, such as the snare and cymbals.

On an electric guitar, muting the low strings and giving a hard muted strum on the neck will give a nice, deep percussive sound. You can also hit the strings with a flat palm in different parts of the guitar neck for sound variations.

Guitar Drums on an Electric Guitar

 Electric Guitar Drum Set Sounds

Track 40

To imitate the low sounds, on an acoustic guitar we can hit the guitar with our hands on the back, sides, or bottom of the instrument. Knocking or tapping with the palms, the knuckles, or the sides of the fist can give many different types of low drum-type sounds.

 Acoustic Guitar Drum Set Sounds

Track 41

Guitar Drums on an Acoustic Guitar

Tip: If you turn up the reverb, you will really hear this effect.

For high-pitched sounds, resting the fingers on the strings and playing string percussion near the bridge will produce a great snare imitation. On an electric guitar, try using the bridge pickup for the most definition on the high sounds.

Tip: Try a few simple drum grooves on the guitar. When you get comfortable, try more complex grooves and fills. Just like anything else you practice, start simple and slow with these drum grooves and gradually add variations and speed.

4.5. Slap Guitar

Though conceived as a technique for electric bass guitar, the **slap technique** can be achieved on a regular guitar by smacking the thumb down on any given string to get a nice slapping sound. Try to position the thumb so that the hard joint strikes the string and make sure you quickly bounce off of it (don't stop on the string). This will work best on the E and A strings.

Although slap guitar works on the same principal as slap bass, because of the smaller distances between the strings, some techniques are more challenging.

Exercises

1. Another bass technique is to place the thumb of your strumming hand underneath the low E string and gently touch the string. Then pull up hard and quick so that the string reaches as far as it will go before it slips off the pad of your thumb and "pops" back down. Try this with a few notes on the lower strings and some groovy lines.

2. Now try placing the pad of your index finger on the underside of the D string. Pull up hard and let the string slap back down. Try alternating the thumb slap of the E string and the finger slap of the D string. You can even add in one of the open strings for a great triplet effect.

On Track 42, you'll hear many of these individual techniques demonstrated, followed by Example 26. In the notation, "S" indicates a note slapped by the thumb, and "P" indicates a note popped by the index finger.

 a) Slapping Notes and Popping, b) Slapping Notes, c) Slapping a Melody

Track 42

Example 26

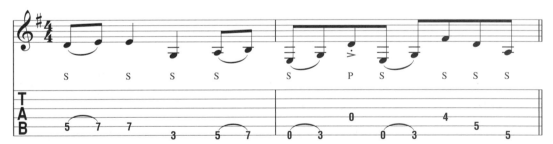

Tips:

- While learning this technique, it's useful to rest your palm against the body of the guitar. A good sound will be produced with a quick rotation of the wrist with a lot of power behind your hit.
- By combining these techniques, you can get a large variety of slapping effects on the guitar.
- If you use some compression or delay, you will get even more "pop" to your sounds.
- Check out Larry Graham, Victor Wooten, and Marcus Miller for some great bass examples; Regi Wooten is pretty incredible on the slap guitar.

4.6. Non-Traditional Objects on Strings

Almost anything can be used to create a unique sound on a guitar! Some objects have been used commonly enough that they deserve to be mentioned here.

Pencil Percussion

Pen or Pencil

The pen or pencil makes a great percussive sound on the guitar. Hold it by one end and let the pen drop on the strings or swing it quickly against the strings.

 Pencil on Strings

Track 43

Example 27

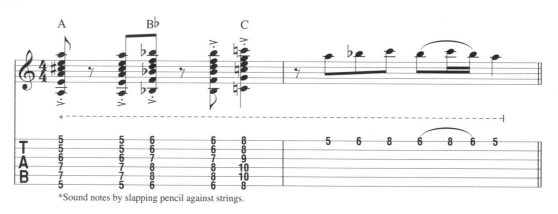

*Sound notes by slapping pencil against strings.

You can let the pen bounce one time or multiple times for a drum roll-type effect. The greatest characteristic of this technique is that you can strike all the strings together. It is a very pianistic effect—similar to the way a piano player is able to rhythmically play a chord.

Tip: This technique is great for chords, but you can use it on single notes as well.

Drum Stick

Use the drum stick exactly the same way as described for the pencil. The added weight and power of the drumstick gives the effect even more drama.

 Hitting Strings with a Drum Stick

Track 44

Violin Bow

Made famous by Jimmy Page, the violin bow seeks to duplicate violin technique on the guitar. It takes some practice, but if you apply the perfect amount of pressure at the right angle (almost parallel to the frets with a slight angle toward the neck) you can get that pristine sustain on the guitar strings. By moving back and forth across the strings, you can get one of the lower strings or even a whole chord to sustain.

Violin Bow on Strings

 Violin Bow on Guitar Strings: a) Chord, b) One String

Track 45

Tips:

- Put rosin on the violin bow, and be generous; around 14 slides (across the rosin cake) will work. Also remember to clean your strings afterward!

- You will also need to tweak all your EQ settings on amps and pedals to accommodate for the wildly different tonal quality of the bowed sound.

- Check out Eddie Phillips of the Creation or Sigur Rós for additional examples of violin bow usage.

Ebow

Ebow

The **Ebow** is meant to improve on the violin bow/guitar combination. With an electric guitar, place the Ebow on a string above the pickup. It will cause the string to vibrate and build on itself. Then you can use your fretting hand to play notes on that string. The energy of the Ebow will keep the string vibrating indefinitely, so enjoy some fantastic and spacey melodic lines! By varying the distance between the Ebow and the pickup, you will be able to change the dynamics and attack of the sound.

 Ebow Improvisation

Track 46

Prepared Guitar

Prepared guitar is, in its simplest form, anything you add to the guitar to enhance the sound. Try threading small strips of paper, felt, rubber, or plastic through the strings near the bridge of the guitar for some interesting sounds. Experiment with any material you can find and see what sounds the most interesting to your ears. Some musicians, such as Pat Metheny or Trevor Gordon Hall, have conceived custom guitars based on a prepared sound of additional resonant strings or, in Trevor's case, a kalimba. You can add tin foil or a baking pan to get a snare like effect or other objects like moon-gel mounted to the body of the instrument to darken or deaden the sound.

Prepared Guitar

In the following example, two common guitar preparation techniques are utilized: objects on the strings and alternate tunings. The guitar is prepared as follows:

Low E String: Nut on the string, positioned above bridge pickup

A String: Normal

D String: Two small washers on string near the bridge

G String: Tuned to F with small washer near bridge

B String: Tuned to C with rubber band wrapped around the end of the string

High E String: Tuned to D with rubber band wrapped around the end of the string

 Prepared Guitar

Track 47

Note: The following example is written in *transposed notation;* that is to say, it is written as if one were playing a normally tuned guitar. The written notes do not match the sounded pitches, but rather what a guitarist would play to get the desired sound. This makes the music far easier to read.

Example 28

Tuning:
(low to high) E-A-D-F-C-D

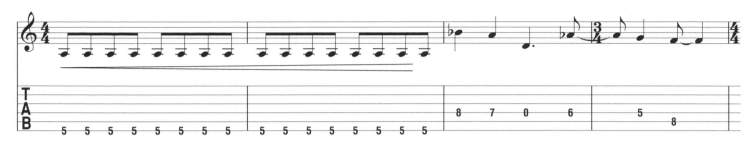

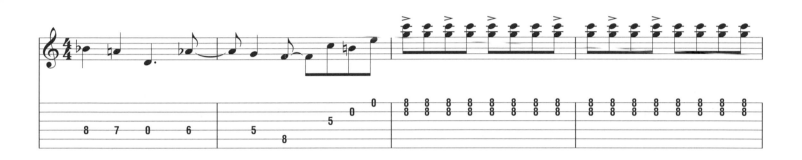

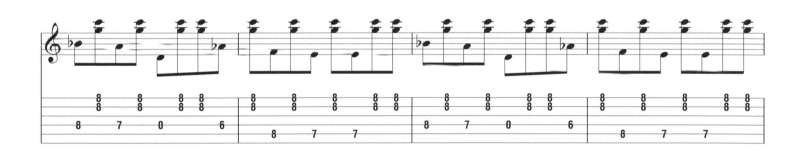

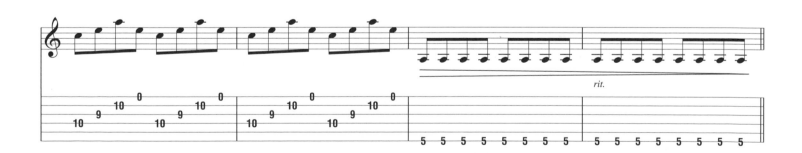

Part II: Plugged Effects
Chapter 5: Wave-Based Effects

5.1. Compression

Compression is likely the most commonly used audio effect. It is used on everything from recorded music to broadcasting, film, television, video games, and even cellular phones! When applied to guitar, compression usually takes the form of an effect pedal, a larger rack mounted unit, or software that models the physical devices.

Compression takes an audio signal and diminishes it at its loudest points. It can also boost the volume level of softer sounds in order to make them louder. The result is that the audio will have a smaller dynamic range than it had before compression was applied.

When you apply compression, the signal is **grabbed**, **held**, and **released**. The effect is applied while the signal is held, and most compressors can be set to grab, hold, or release the signal at a particular level of volume.

The result of all this has two manifestations for guitar. The first is that it will even out the dynamics of anything that is played. For example, a fingerstyle guitar part will sound clearer because the soft notes will be heard more easily. A strumming or funk rhythm part will sound more even and may groove harder. Secondly, with compression, it is possible to give notes greater sustain due to the evening of the dynamic signal.

These benefits come at the expense of having less expressive dynamics in the sound. Small inflections may be minimized by the compression effect. Compression and its uses take time to master, and experimentation is essential.

 Funk Rhythm Part Before and After Compression

Track 48

Example 29

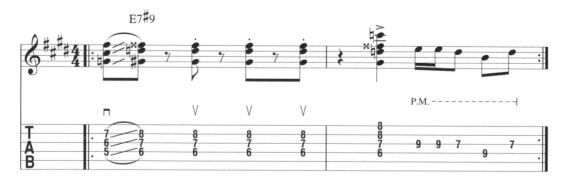

Tips:

- Try many combinations of the compression parameters, such as attack, hold, gain, volume, and tone.
- Use compression on an acoustic guitar by running the sound through a PA system or a recording rig.

Compression is also a useful and distinct sound on acoustic guitars.

Acoustic Guitar Before and After Compression

Track 49

Example 30

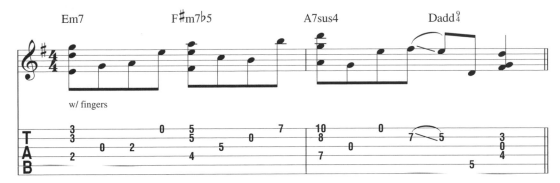

Note: Almost all recorded music is compressed in some way, so mastery of this effect will certainly lead to more professional-sounding recordings.

5.2. Overdrive, Distortion, and Fuzz

Perhaps the "original" guitar effect, this sound is instantly recognizable and has defined generations of musical styles. Overdrive happens when an input device (such as an electric guitar) sends too much power (signal) into an output device (such as a tube amplifier). When that happens, the audio wave gets **clipped**—shortened or chopped off—because the output cannot match the input.

We experience this phenomenon as a distorted signal—that wonderful overdriven, crunchy sound. Naturally, the more power applied going in, the heavier and smoother that overdriven sound will become.

Different Degrees of Overdrive

Track 50

You can achieve overdrive by using an amplifier and increasing the volume (thus signal level) to the extreme. On amplifiers that have a master volume, keep the master low so as to not blow out your ears! Overdrive pedals also send more signal to the amplifier and usually come with their own built-in master volume.

Note: Volume or **gain** control how much signal is pumped into the amplifier, and **master volume** controls the absolute volume of the sound.

Digital simulations of overdrive have gotten better over the years, and they are worth experimenting with, especially in recording situations. It is helpful to understand what the simulation represents.

Overdrive vs. Distortion vs. Fuzz

Simply put, **overdrive** is a naturally-occurring clipping of the wave by increasing the power level and volume. **Distortion** is a forced clipping of the wave without adding power. Most overdrive pedals and sounds are actually technically distortion effects, but the sounds can be so similar, it can be hard to differentiate. At a lower setting, distortion can sound like overdrive, but distortion is usually a "heavier" sound than overdrive and includes more EQ and compression embedded in the pathway.

Fuzz is a variation on distortion using artificial signal clipping, and it has its own set of unique characteristics. It can be a creamier or sharper sound than distortion.

 a) Clean, b) Overdrive, c) Fuzz, d) Distortion

Track 51

Example 31

Tip: Experiment with different combinations of amps, pedals, and digital modeling until you find the sounds you like the most. You will always discover something new in this category of effects.

Famous Recordings Featuring Overdrive, Fuzz, and Distortion:
- Rolling Stones – "(I Can't Get No) Satisfaction"
- Cream – "Sunshine of Your Love"
- Metallica – "Enter Sandman"
- Nirvana – "Smells Like Teen Spirit"

Chapter 6: Time-Based Effects

6.1. Reverb

Reverb is one of the guitarist's most useful effects because it deepens and lengthens the sound of the instrument. Reverb happens when many reflections (or echoes) of a sound build up and are heard after the initial sound occurs. You will experience natural reverb if you play anywhere with a large resonant space. Several types of reverb have been used frequently in live situations and on recordings:

- **Spring reverb** is created by running the sound through a metal spring and capturing it on the other end (with a small pickup). This sound is added to the original sound. Many amplifiers use spring reverb, and many reverb pedals and digital reverb simulators include a spring reverb setting.

- **Plate reverb** uses the same concept as the spring reverb but runs the sound through a large, suspended metal plate. It is a distinct sound, and most digital emulators include a plate reverb setting.

- **Digital reverbs** are computer simulations of spring or plate reverbs, or they are simulations of different rooms. Increasingly sophisticated digital reverbs can simulate buildings, famous performance spaces, vintage amplifiers, and other gear.

 Short and Long Chords Using: a) Spring Reverb, b) Plate Reverb, c) Chamber, d) Very Large Chamber ("Ambience")

Track 52

When setting digital reverbs, you are able to control the time before the reverb is heard (known as **pre-delay**), the amount of reverb added, how long it lasts, and even some EQ options for a brighter or darker reverb tone.

6.2. Delay

A **delay effect** is any effect that copies the input sound and repeats it after the original sound. Delay can be achieved by analog or digital methods, but in either case the effect works by recording the original sound and then playing it back based on parameters selected by the user.

- **Tape delay** was the original form of a delay effect. The audio was recorded on magnetic tape and then played back.

- **Digital delay** provides the same effect using circuitry in the place of tape.

- **Reverse** delay plays the input sound backwards as an output sound. This can be a wonderfully spooky effect.

Most delay pedals and units allow you to choose settings such as the amount of repetitions, the rate of decay, and the volume of the delay sound relative to the input volume. Some more advanced units allow you to alter the tone of the delay or combine effects.

Delay simulators are digital units that emulate specific types of delay such as tape delay (a warm sound with specific decay rates) and well-known standard delays based on famous recordings.

 a) Delay Setting 1, b) Delay Setting 2, c) Delay Setting 3, d) Reverse Delay
Track 53

Example 32

Famous Recordings Featuring Delay:
- Pink Floyd – "Run Like Hell"
- Van Halen – "Cathedral"
- U2 – "Where the Streets Have No Name"

Often multiple delays are used in tandem to give a very thick sound or texture. Check out U2's *Joshua Tree* album for some excellent examples of single and multiple delays.

 Multiple Delays: a) One Note, b) Example 32
Track 54

Note: In the recording studio or for live performance, the speed of delay can be synchronized to the tempo of the song (such as in "Where the Streets Have No Name" or "Cathedral") or allowed to be out of sync with the tempo (such as in Pat Metheny's "Bright Size Life").

6.3. Loops

A **loop** is a specific kind of delay, in which there is a very long delay time and the original sound is repeated until you turn it off. The most unique feature of the loop effect is the ability to layer sounds on top of the others.

To achieve this effect, first play a short riff into the loop device. Then, as the loop device continues to repeat your first idea, play a second idea complementary to the first. You should then be able to hear both of your ideas played simultaneously. You can continue this process indefinitely.

The following example is a five-part loop, intended to be constructed one layer at a time and then improvised over.

 Five-Part Loop

Track 55

Example 33

Some newer loop units can record for a very long time, so it is possible to create loops that last for the entire length of the song or performance. The best way to learn how to use the loop pedal is through experimentation, so keep an open mind and always try new things. You will be continually inspired by this effect.

Tip: Try listening to some guitarists who use loops very well, such as Pat Metheny (check out his recording of Steve Reich's "Electric Counterpoint"), Steve Morse, The Edge, Brian May on live Queen recordings, and modern singer-songwriters like Jason Mraz and Howie Day.

6.4. Tremolo

Tremolo is a time effect that oscillates volume. The input sound is run through some type of oscillating device, which is usually either a low frequency oscillator or a digital simulation of one. This means that the volume of the sound will increase and decrease at a regular rate.

Note: With regards to audio effects, tremolo is an oscillation of volume. **Vibrato** is an oscillation of pitch.

Tremolo effects are built into some amplifiers, and there are also pedal tremolos and digital simulations embedded in recording software.

The key parameter while using tremolo is the **rate**. A slower rate, like delay, will add depth and sustain, while a faster rate can add a shimmering effect. Advanced tremolos may have a tone control to alter the brightness of the tremolo sound. Some tremolos also have a **depth** or **intensity** control, which determines how far the volume decreases each time.

 Tremolo: a) One Note, b) Chords

Track 56

Exercise

Experiment with setting the tremolo rate as a subdivision of the tempo of the song. Eighth notes or triplets work particularly well.

Famous Recordings Featuring Tremolo:
- Tommy James and the Shondells – "Crimson and Clover"
- Green Day – "Boulevard of Broken Dreams"
- Everly Brothers – "All I Have to Do Is Dream"

Chapter 7: Modulation Effects

7.1. Vibrato

Vibrato works on the same premise as the tremolo effect except instead of an oscillation of volume, vibrato is an oscillation of pitch. In contrast to the vibrato discussed earlier that is created by the hands, electric vibrato is created using analog or digital equipment. The advantage of this kind of vibrato is that you can use it for chords or passages in which finger vibrato would be very difficult. You can also set the vibrato rate to a particular tempo.

Like tremolo, a good vibrato pedal or digital simulator will allow you to determine the rate (how fast the pitch changes), the depth (how far the pitch is sliding from the original note), and the decay (how long the vibrato lasts). You can set the vibrato to emulate a finger vibrato or, by using the more extreme settings, you can achieve some non-conventional sounds.

 a) Vibrato Chords Using Different Settings, b) Melody

Track 57

Example 34

Some guitars use a whammy bar to create a vibrato effect. Playing while using the whammy bar creates a sliding sound. The pitches move up and down almost randomly in relation to your fretted note. It can even be compared to sliding on a violin or a Theremin.

7.2. Chorus

The **chorus** effect is a very common guitar effect that gives a shiny and glimmering tone. Chorus has two components that are combined to create the sound. The first is a very short delay. The delay is so short that it blends with the original (input) sound. The second component of the chorus is an oscillator that changes the delay time enough to alter the pitch of the affected sound. This is why chorus sounds "out of tune." The original pitch is thickened, like a choir, by the addition of the slightly detuned sound.

 Chorus: a) Chord, Scale, Example 34 Using One Pedal, b) Same on Different Chorus Pedal

Track 58

Chorus is usually created by pedals or software simulators, though some amplifiers have digital built-in chorus effects. Most choruses (like delays) will allow you to choose the **rate** (how fast), the **depth** (how out of tune), and the **thickness** (volume of the detuned sound).

Famous Recordings Featuring Chorus:
- Mike Stern – "Wishing Well"
- Live – "Selling the Drama"
- Nirvana – "Come as You Are"

7.3. Pitch Shifters

Pitch shifting is any type of effect meant to detune the instrument. Some common pitch shifters are whammy pedals, octave pedals, and harmonizers.

Whammy pedals will provide the same effect as a whammy bar, usually with more control and parameter choices. By stepping on the pedal or holding it, the pitch of your input sound will bend up or down to a specified interval.

 Whammy Pedal Improvisation, Set to Octave Above

Track 59

An **octave pedal** simply copies the input pitch and outputs a pitch one octave away (usually down). Octave pedals allow you to control the register, the volume of the output sound, and some even include a slight fuzz or distortion effect. Octave effects are a great way to thicken a line or make something much more powerful. Be careful using this effect on chords, however, as the intonation might not be great.

 Octave Pedal: a) Octave Below, b) Octave Above, c) Octave Below and Above Improvisation

Track 60

Harmonizers provide the same effect as the octave pedal, but instead of merely one octave they can generate any interval relative to the input sound. Some harmonizers allow you to choose a major or minor key and generate intervals diatonic to only that key. More sophisticated harmonizers can even do full triads or seventh chords based on a pre-selected mode and your input pitch.

Like the octave pedal, a harmonizer can usually control the relative volume of the intervals, the key, and potentially a tone modifier choosing either a bright or a dark variation of the output sound.

 Harmonizer: a) Major 3rd, b) Perfect 5th, c) Minor 7th

Track 61

Example 35

Chapter 8: Filter Effects

8.1. Flanger

Flanging is a complex effect that produces the sound of a "swoosh" or breath. It sounds great on all sorts of guitar parts. In its simplest form, the input sound is copied, delayed ever so slightly, and mixed with the input sound. The copied sound is hooked into a filter that passes through the frequency spectrum, accentuating some frequencies and not others. The end result is you will hear major alterations in the tone of the final output sound, alternating from very dark to very thin and bright.

Flanger pedals and their digital simulators can control the speed of the alteration (rate), how dramatic the frequencies change (depth), and the volume of the affected signal. At low settings, the flanger can add body to a sound. At higher depth and volume settings, the flanger can sound otherworldly! Track 62 demonstrates the sound of a flanger on one chord and then with Example 3, played a bit freely to accentuate the effect.

 Flanger: a) One Chord, b) Example 3

Track 62

Famous Recordings Featuring Flangers:
- Van Halen – "Unchained"
- Lenny Kravitz – "Are You Gonna Go My Way"

8.2. Phaser

A **phaser** is similar to a flanger except for the exclusion of delay in the signal. In a phaser, the input signal is split. One half of the input signal is sent through a filter and then blended back with the original sound. Because there is no delay, this results in the filter sweeping through frequencies, and the input and output sounds will alternate between being "in phase" and "out of phase." This gives a peak and valley effect that is powerful and ethereal.

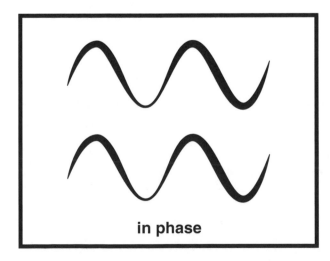

in phase

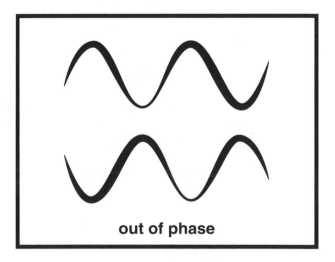

out of phase

Compare this with the flanger to really hear the sonic impact of in- and out-of-phase frequencies. Phaser pedals and simulators usually include the familiar rate, depth, and volume controls found on most types of filter-based pedals.

 Phaser: a) One Chord, b) Example 3

Track 63

Famous Recordings Featuring Phasers:
- Live – "Lightning Crashes"
- Radiohead – "Paranoid Android"
- Pink Floyd – "Have a Cigar"

8.3. Wah Wah

Wah wah is a frequency filter that usually can be controlled by the player in real time. When using a manual wah pedal, rocking the pedal back and forth filters the low or high frequencies out of the sound, resulting in a drastic brightening or darkening of the tone. Using an auto wah effect, the frequency filter becomes automated and can be set based on a tempo.

 Wah Wah: a) One Chord, b) Muted Scratches, c) Funk Grooves

Track 64

Exercises
- Use the wah pedal to accentuate certain notes in a melody or beats in a rhythmic pattern.
- Rock the pedal to a steady beat and make a strumming rhythm groove to your wah tempo.

Famous Recordings Featuring Wah Wah:
- Jimi Hendrix – "Voodoo Child (Slight Return)"
- Blind Faith – "Presence of the Lord"
- Cream – "White Room"
- Guns N' Roses – "Sweet Child O' Mine"

8.4. Volume Swells

Though technically not a filter effect, the **volume swell** is based on alternation between loud and soft. By using the volume control on the guitar itself, or a designated volume pedal, you can sweep between full volume, a loud sound, a soft volume, and no volume.

 Volume Swell: a) Crescendo, b) Decrescendo, c) Oscillation, d) Melody

Track 65

Tip: One very calming effect is to play a chord with the volume pedal depressed, giving no volume to the attack of the sound, and then slowly swell up the volume for a fade-in effect. Compression and a healthy delay or reverb will heighten the effect.

Chapter 9: Effects Layering

9.1. Common Combinations

With so many effects out there, it is easy to get lost with regards to which ones to choose and how to arrange and combine them. As a general rule, when combining effects and layering pedals, it is important to know which effects you are actually going to use. Also, set up the order of the effects based on how the end result should sound. For example, if you have a wah wah pedal and a delay, you can either *delay* the wah sound (wah wah first) or *wah* the delay sound (delay first).

Tip: It will take time and experimentation to develop your own preferences and techniques. However, as a place to start, try arranging your effects like this:

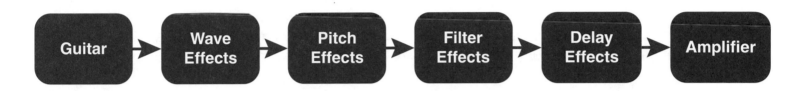

In the following track, these common combinations are played using the same music.

Track 66

a) Delay and Chorus, b) Delay and Distortion, c) Distortion and Wah, d) Delay and Phaser, e) Overdrive and Chorus

Example 36

9.2. Unique Combinations

Some less standard but beautiful sounds can be created as well. Track 67 demonstrates some other combinations using Example 36.

Track 67

a) Delay with Second Delay and Chorus, b) Phaser and Overdrive, c) Tremolo with Distortion and Delay, d) Flanger and Distortion

9.3. Special Sounds

A **ring modulator** is an alien-sounding effect that mixes a volume alteration with frequency filters and frequency blending. This effect is marvelous and endlessly fascinating.

Ring Modulator: a) Chord, b) Scale, c) Example 36

Track 68

Tip: Try combining a ring modulator with delay and overdrive.

Amp modeling is an increasingly popular technology, the principal being a digital simulation of the circuitry and speakers of well-known amplifiers. Depending on your personal preferences and how much equipment you want to carry around, amp modelers can be a great-sounding way to have a large sound palette at your fingertips.

For the sake of comparison in the book, we have used a digital model of a very similar type of amplifier heard on the previous tracks, with the exact same settings. For more details on the equipment used on this recording, see the **Gear List** in the Appendix.

Amp Modeling: a) Example 26, b) Example 32, c) Example 34, d) Example 36

Track 69

Amp Settings

Digital Amp Model Settings

Other special sounds can be achieved using **guitar synthesizers** and **MIDI** (Musical Instrument Digital Interface).

Part III: Recording Studio Experiments
Chapter 10: Studio Effects

This section is intended to provide some "seed" ideas for your recording sessions—some common and some less commonly used techniques. The recording studio is best thought of as an instrument unto itself, and like any instrument (or any technique in this book), it takes practice to achieve a desired sound. All musicians should strive to develop some fluency in the recording studio, but it is expected that other specialists, such as engineers and producers, will be studio collaborators and can assist you in your sonic experiments. What follows are some techniques that are specific to guitar in a recording studio environment.

10.1. Overdubs and Sound Layers

One of the most frequently used studio techniques is **overdubbing**—the practice of stacking guitar parts in order to create a thickened texture. Here are some considerations for arranging multiple guitars...

Rhythm and Divisions of the Pulse

* To thicken a texture, make sure not every part has the same rhythm. For example, one part in half notes and one part in eighth notes will have a thick sound without interfering.

Register

* What are the *highest* and *lowest* notes of each guitar part? Do they overlap? It is helpful to "map out" guitar parts on a grand staff, just as one would when arranging orchestral instruments.

* **Density** of each part: how many notes is each guitar sounding?

* **Combinations of guitars, amps, and pickups**: As a general rule, multiple guitars and amplifiers should be layered using *different* equipment. For example, if one track is played on an electric guitar with single coil pickups, a second part could be played on an instrument with humbucking pickups. This gives a more textured sound than using the same exact guitar for multiple parts.

* Just as with pickups, using multiple amplifiers on a track gives a greater sonic richness to layered guitars.

* Timbres that sound good by themselves (think effects like chorus or overdrive) do not always sound good **blended**, so it is important to track new parts while listening to existing ones, thereby making sure the tones complement one another.

* Never underestimate the power of acoustic guitars! This includes doubling an electric part or as textures unto themselves. As with electrics, multiple acoustics blended sound thicker than the same instrument on multiple parts.

 Acoustic Guitar Part Doubled with Electric Guitar Part

Track 70

10.2. Microphone Techniques and Distances – Spatial Sound Effects

Experimenting with microphone distance is a great way to literally add dimension to your sound. Placing mics far from your instrument or amp can give a more live feeling, whereas closer distances will give a more isolated sound. Throughout this book, each track has used a "medium" microphone distance of 1.5 feet. The following track showcases the same music using close and far microphone placement.

Track 71

a) Microphone Distance 1 Foot: Examples 26 and 36, b) Microphone Distance 5 Feet: Examples 26 and 36

10.3. Non-Traditional Sound Design (Cars, Animals, Landscapes)

Though normally a film soundtrack technique, **sound design** is a growing field and refers to acoustically recording sounds that are not traditional instruments. Through use of MIDI, however, these sounds can be played on a synth guitar and incorporated into your music. Sound libraries often include nature and urban sounds for this exact purpose.

Part IV: Avant Garde
Chapter 11: Unusual Sounds

11.1. Extreme Effects

Extreme effects can be created in a myriad of ways, but some striking results can come from layering and shaping studio sounds. In the following track, three short improvisations were played through an amplifier using a clean tone. Then various studio plugins were added to create layer and dimension. This technique can be a guitarist's and producer's goldmine of new and exotic sounds, and often a more dimensional sound can be created in a digital studio this way.

 a) Eventide H3000 + Phaser + Delay + Reverb, b) Distorted Signal in Parallel with Dry Signal + Two Delays, c) Random Delay + Unfiltered Audio

Track 72

11.2. Unorthodox Stringing Techniques

Simply put, this technique involves changing the order and type of guitar strings used to create some unique tuning and voicing combinations. In the following track, the guitar was strung as such (low to high):

- **Low E String Position**: E string tuned to E♭
- **A String Position**: E string tuned to A♭
- **D String Position**: G string tuned to A♭ (octave higher)
- **G String Position**: B string tuned to B♭
- **B String Position**: B string tuned to C
- **High E String Position**: E string tuned to D

 a) Unique String Combination, b) Improvisation Using This Tuning

Track 73

11.3. Designing Instruments and Guitar Modifications

Guitarists from Keith Richards to Prince to Pat Metheny have experimented with designing experimental instruments, the most formidable and exotic example being the latter's "Orchestrion" project.

Here are some simple modifications you can experiment with, even if you are not a guitar luthier:

- Changing pickups
- Stringing combinations
- Integrating MIDI technology
- Removing/adding frets
- Changing outputs
- Prepared guitar

Part V: Etudes

1. Delicate

This Etude utilizes the open strings and the natural harmonics of the guitar. Because of the standard tuning, this etude has a pentatonic, modal, and almost impressionistic quality. Notice the wide lush voicings in measure 8 that demonstrate a great way to use open strings on the guitar. This little song suggests an innocent pastoral quality; I imagine a man calling his young daughter to come inside on a summer day. The harmonics at the end suggest a child's voice. Keep in mind that several fingerings are possible for the open-string measures. Definitely play this one rubato and be gentle with each phrase.

Track 74

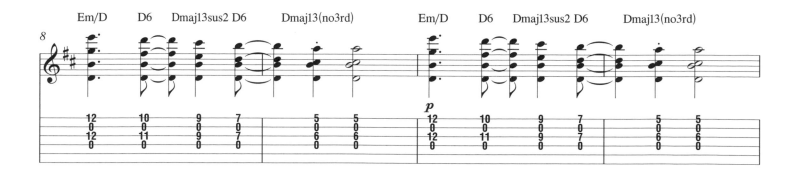

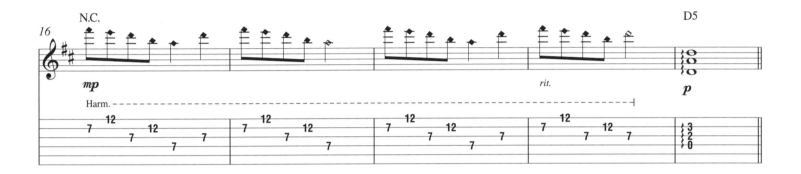

2. Walk to Run

This etude features several extremely useful techniques and two different rhythmic feels. It has a bluesy, riffy vibe that makes use of bends and pentatonics, as well as single-note palm muting. The second section morphs into a heavy rock feel, with palm-muted dyads and some loud sus2 chords. Try to get the whole piece to sound smooth—especially the transition between the two feels. Remember that vibrato on each string will sound different, so experiment with alternative fingerings to your liking.

Track 75

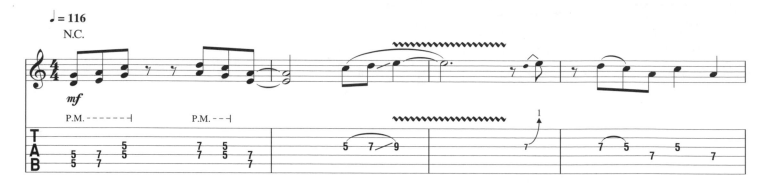

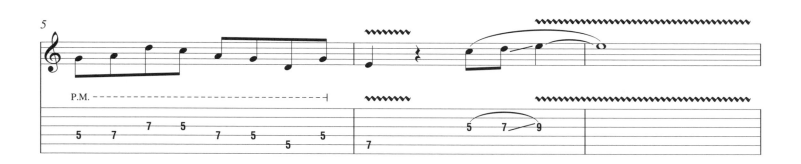

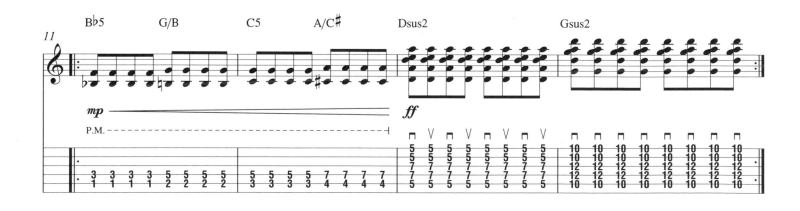

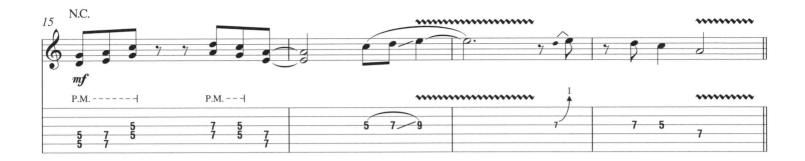

3. Rain

This etude showcases DADGAD tuning—one of the most popular alternate tunings—and use of the slide, which sounds particularly great against low open strings. The middle section of the piece highlights some intriguing voicing possibilities that come from alternate tunings. Try the slide on the ring or little finger so that your other fingers can jump on to the fretted section. A fingerstyle or hybrid right hand may make this etude easier and the parts more clear. Try it slow for a bluesy sound, or even try the slide section rubato!

Track 76

DADGAD tuning:
(low to high) D-A-D-G-A-D

♩ = 90

N.C.(Dm)

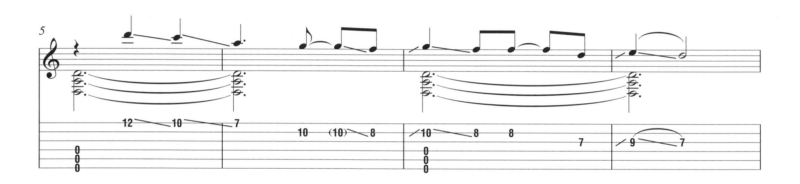

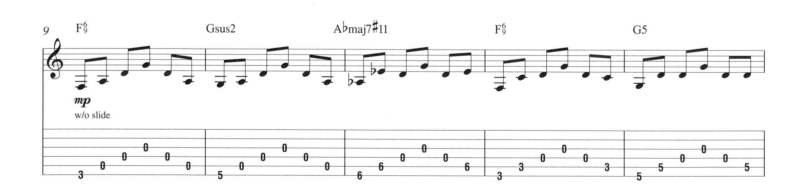

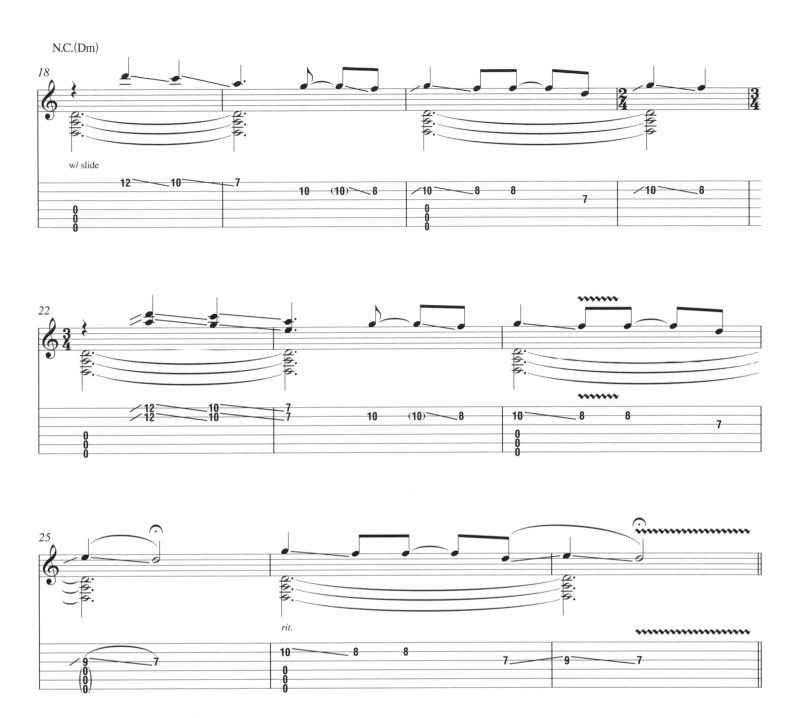

4. Shadow Dance

This slightly trickier etude combines tapping, hammer-ons, pull-offs, and some string percussion. You can slap the strings with your right hand and always have the left hand prepared in the proper position for the next note. For measures 10 and 14, try just the slightest bit of left-hand pressure to get a faint hint of the correct pitch. For a legato feel, try to make the tapped lines smooth and even—i.e., balance the volume of the taps, hammer-ons, pull-offs, and open strings for one smooth line.

5. Please Stay

This etude, body drumming included, is typical of a folky or pop guitar part. Try playing this on an acoustic guitar with a touch of delay to really hear it. For the body drumming, you may want to keep the pick in your strumming hand or just be able to grab it when needed. You can also try this entire etude fingerstyle. Remember that you'll get different sounds with the guitar drumming depending on whether you use the palm of the hand, a closed fist, or even two or three fingers. Capos are wonderful for their ability to give the guitar a more harp-like sound in every key, especially higher on the neck. Transpose this etude to the seventh fret for a very shiny, bright sound!

6. Time In

This etude with a funky groove is a prime candidate for the use of compression. It makes the single-note lines really stand out and groove harder. Not to mention, the muted scratching balances much better when using compression than without it. Volume swells are a classic electric technique that is common in many styles. Practice this by setting for yourself how many beats it should take to go from zero sound to full volume. Try swelling each chord in four beats or two chords over eight beats (hard!). Make sure the volume is all the way up by the time you get to measure 21 so you can throw the compression back on!

Track 79

♩ = 90

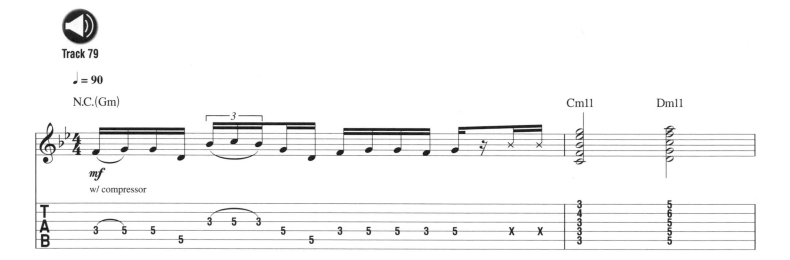

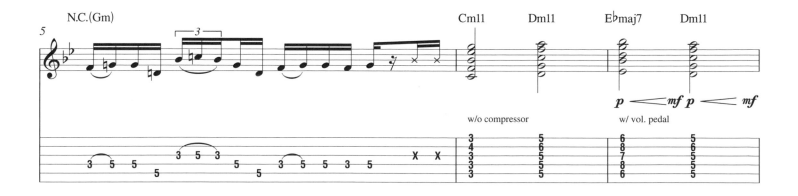

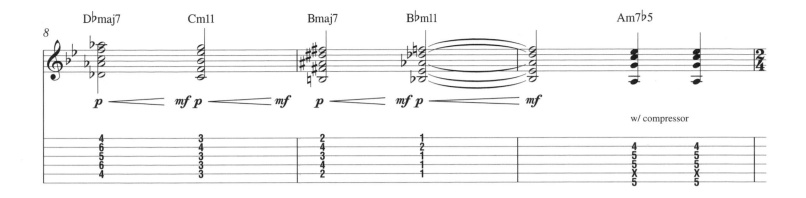

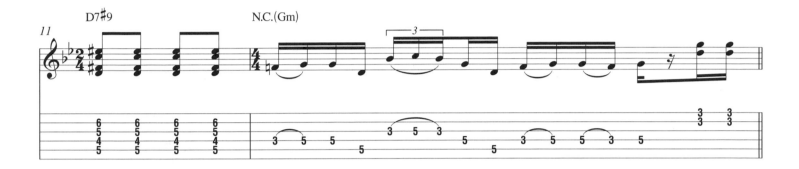

7. Bird Songs

Loop technology is an amazing way to make music and is constantly evolving. For this etude, we are stacking loops in tempo, so it's a good idea to practice setting up a steady pulse; even practicing with a metronome is helpful when rehearsing loop performances. Make sure each layer is grooving well before adding the next one—and feel free to add your own! Some advanced loopers have relative volume controls, which can be extremely useful when crafting a sound or texture. Lastly, set your delay so that it is in sync with your loop time. That way everything will sound good when the loop recycles, and it won't "hiccup." The best loops are ones you can't even tell are loops!

Track 80

8. Jazz Hard

This etude is typical of a hard rock or prog rock guitar part, alternating from open strings to palm muting to single notes and false harmonics and back. It's important to develop fluency in these techniques and the ability to switch between them seamlessly. Because of the higher gain, playing with distortion demands more technique and control from the player than when playing with a clean sound. Try many variations of drive and distortion for this etude. (Hint: The heavier the sound, the greater the challenge!)

Track 81

9. Ocean Lights

This etude, a study in stacking effects, is another example of an arena rock-type guitar part. The goal is clarity of the part and creating a sound that is powerful and pleasing. Tone control will make a big difference here, as will type of guitar and type of pickups. Try this etude on different instruments or through different amps and pedals. Also check out the difference in picking this near the neck and near the bridge. You can grab a huge degree of extra tonal variation by changing your strumming position.

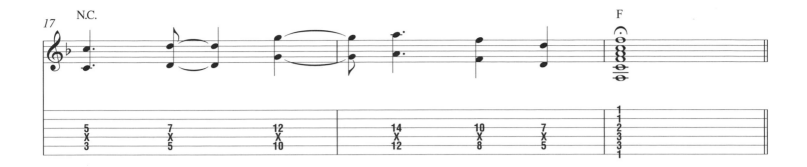

10. Exit

This last etude has a funky, bluesy vibe, using the wah wah and pitch shifter for some classic '70s-type sounds. Make sure you play the "and" of beat 2 as an upstroke for the proper wah sting. You can rock the wah to the tempo or manipulate it so that it is on the treble side when you want accents and on the bass side otherwise. Either way is quite effective, but for this piece I would rock the pedal in half notes; that should place the accents in the right spots. The pitch shifter is really great here because it gives weight to the lines. Just be sure to turn it off before you transition to playing chords, as some pitch shifters do not intonate multiple notes well.

Afterword

"Every sound is a song"

–Joe Zawinul

Sometimes the most important job of the musician is to stay inspired, continue learning, and keep their musical channel open. We hope the topics in this book can be jumping off points for new ideas, new ways to practice, new songs, new performance ideas, and new compositional techniques. The guitar is a simple and old instrument that has become ubiquitous in popular music around the world. Its innovators have shaped music as we know it, and we hope that this book can shed light on some of their secrets.

Thank you for joining us on this journey into the many sides of the contemporary guitar. We hope you have found something to take home with you.

Appendix

Recommended Listening

For this list we have included both specific tracks and, where applicable, names of guitarists who frequently use a particular technique throughout their playing.

Nylon String Guitar

- **Classical:** Manuel Barrueco – "12 Spanish Dances"
- **Pop:** Enrique Iglesias – "Bailamos"
- **Bossa Nova:** Charlie Byrd – "Girl From Ipanema"
- **Classical guitarists to check out:** Andrés Segovia, Julian Bream, John Williams

Steel String Acoustic Guitar

- Leo Kottke – "The Fisherman"
- Al Di Meola and Paco de Lucia – "Mediterranean Sundance"
- James Taylor – "Fire and Rain"

Electric Guitars

- Jimmy Page (Led Zeppelin) – "Stairway to Heaven"
- Eric Clapton (Cream) – "Crossroads"

Single Coil Pickups

- Jimi Hendrix – "Little Wing"
- Stevie Ray Vaughan – "Texas Flood"

Humbucking Pickups

- Les Paul – "How High the Moon"
- Slash (Guns N' Roses) – "Sweet Child O' Mine"

Fretless Guitar
- David Fiuczynski – "Lullaby for Che"
- Bumblefoot – "Mafalda"

Guitar Synth
- Pat Metheny – "Question and Answer (Live)," "Are You Going With Me"
- Jimmy Page – "Who's to Blame"

Steel Pan
- Alex Burns – "Que Vuelva"
- Dire Straits – *Brothers in Arms* (whole album)

Tube Amplifers
- Eric Clapton (Derek & the Dominos) – "Layla"
- Jeff Beck – "Cause We've Ended as Lovers"
- Allan Holdsworth – "Secrets"

Solid-State Amplifers
- Allan Holdsworth – *One of a Kind* (Bill Bruford album)
- Iron Maiden – "Seventh Son of a Seventh Son"

Harmonics
- Jeff Beck – "Where Were You" (and whammy bar)
- Lenny Breau and Tal Farlow – *Chance Meeting* (whole album)

Bends
- Stevie Ray Vaughan – "Texas Flood"
- Steve Vai – *Passion and Warfare* (whole album)

Vibrato
- Eric Clapton
- John Williams
- Jeff Beck
- B.B. King

Whammy Bar

- Jeff Beck – "A Day in the Life"
- Duane Eddy – "Rebel Rouser"
- Steve Vai – *Passion and Warfare* (whole album)
- Joe Satriani – *Surfing with the Alien* (whole album)

Slide Guitar

- Duane Allman
- Derek Trucks
- Dave Tronzo

Sweep Picking

- Yngwie Malmsteen
- Frank Gambale
- Jason Becker

Palm Muting

- Green Day – "Basket Case"
- Semisonic – "Closing Time"
- Megadeth – *Rust in Peace* (whole album)

Open Strings

- Bill Frisell
- Tommy Emmanuel
- Alex Hutchings
- Leo Kottke
- Pat Metheny

Capos

For most common usage, check out singer-songwriters such as Paul Simon, Joni Mitchell, and James Taylor.

Alternate Tunings

- Davey Graham
- Andy McKee
- Tony McManus
- Michael Hedges
- Jeff Tweedy (Wilco)
- Thurston Moore (Sonic Youth)

Tapping

- Eddie Van Halen
- Steve Vai
- Stian Westerhus
- Stanley Jordan

Guitar Percussion

- Andy McKee
- Paco de Lucia
- Keith Rowe
- Hans Tammen

Slap Guitar

- Regi Wooten

Avant Garde and Prepared Guitar

- Roger Kleier
- Hans Tammen
- Stian Westerhus
- Fred Frith
- Marc Ribot
- Keith Rowe
- David Torn
- Tom Morello

Gear List

The following gear was used for the audio recordings in this book.

Microphones

All acoustic guitars: Warm Audio WA87

All electric guitars: Neumann TLM 103

Track 1 Nylon, steel, hollow body
   a) Manuel Rodriguez y Jios guitar
   b) Bayard Guitars 00-14
   c) Guild X150 hollow body guitar unplugged
   d) Guild X150 with Fender Twin

Track 2 Single coil pickups
Fender Stratocaster '70s reissue
Fender Twin

Track 3 Humbucking pickups
Gibson SG 2010
Fender Twin

Track 4 Resonator guitar
1929 National
Fender Twin

Track 5 Tube amplifiers
Artinger Custom Guitars
1968 Fender Bassman head
1964 Bandmaster cabinet

Track 6 Solid-state amplifiers
Artinger Custom Guitars
Orange Crush Pro 60

Track 7 Right-hand techniques
Artinger Custom Guitars
1968 Fender Bassman head
1964 Bandmaster cabinet

Track 8 Pick types
Bayard Guitars

Track 9 Tonal variation
Bayard Guitars

Track 10 Natural harmonics
Artinger Custom Guitars
Orange Crush Pro 60

Track 11 Harmonic melody
Artinger Custom Guitars
Orange Crush Pro 60

Track 12 False harmonics
Gibson SG 2010
Orange Crush Pro 60
   a) No distortion
   b) Distortion

Track 13 Harp effect
Gibson SG 2010
Orange Crush Pro 60

Track 14 Bends
Artinger Custom Guitars
1968 Fender Bassman head
1964 Bandmaster cabinet

Track 15 Full guitar bend
Artinger Custom Guitars
1968 Fender Bassman head
1964 Bandmaster cabinet

Track 16 Vibrato
Artinger Custom Guitars
1968 Fender Bassman head
1964 Bandmaster cabinet

Track 17 Whammy bar
Fender Stratocaster '70s reissue
1968 Fender Bassman head
1964 Bandmaster cabinet

Track 18 Slide scale
Fender Stratocaster 1999 American Standard
1968 Fender Bassman head
1964 Bandmaster cabinet

Track 19 Tremolo
Artinger Custom Guitars
1968 Fender Bassman head
1964 Bandmaster cabinet

Track 20 Sweet picking
Artinger Custom Guitars
1968 Fender Bassman head
1964 Bandmaster cabinet

Track 21 Rake
Artinger Custom Guitars
1968 Fender Bassman head
1964 Bandmaster cabinet

Track 22 Palm muting
Artinger Custom Guitars
1968 Fender Bassman head
1964 Bandmaster cabinet

Track 23 Strumming
Bayard Guitars

Track 24 Open strings 1
Artinger Custom Guitars
Fender Twin

Track 25 Open strings 2
Artinger Custom Guitars
Fender Twin

Track 26 Open strings 3
Artinger Custom Guitars
Fender Twin

Track 27 Open strings 4
Artinger Custom Guitars
Fender Twin

Track 28 Open strings 5
Artinger Custom Guitars
Fender Twin

Track 29 Capos 1
Artinger Custom Guitars
Fender Twin

Track 30 Capos 2
Artinger Custom Guitars
Fender Twin

Track 31 Capos 3
Artinger Custom Guitars
Fender Twin

Track 32 Tunings
Taylor GS Mini

Track 33 Tapping 1
Artinger Custom Guitars
Fender Twin

Track 34 Tapping 2
Artinger Custom Guitars
Fender Twin

Track 35 Tapping 3
Artinger Custom Guitars
Fender Twin

Track 36 Tapping 4
Artinger Custom Guitars
Fender Twin

Track 37 Pick slides
Artinger Custom Guitars
Fender Twin

Track 38 Engine sounds
Artinger Custom Guitars
Fender Twin
Fulltone Plimsoul Overdrive

Track 39 String percussion
Artinger Custom Guitars
Fender Twin

Track 40 Guitar drums 1
Artinger Custom Guitars
Fender Twin

Track 41 Guitar drums 2
Taylor GS Mini

Track 42 Slap guitar
Artinger Custom Guitars
Fender Twin

Track 43 Objects on strings: pencil
Artinger Custom Guitars
Fender Twin

Track 44 Objects on strings: drumstick
Artinger Custom Guitars
Fender Twin

Track 45 Objects on strings: violin bow
Artinger Custom Guitars
Fender Twin

Track 46 Objects on strings: Ebow
Artinger Custom Guitars
Fender Twin
Pigtronix Fat Drive
MXR Carbon Copy

Track 47 Prepared guitar
Traveler Guitar Sonic L-22
Nuts and bolts
Fender Twin

Track 48 Compression
Artinger Custom Guitar
Fender Twin
Pigtronix Philosopher's Rock Compressor

Track 49 Acoustic studio compression
Bayard Guitars
    a) Compression
    b) No compression

Track 50 Degrees of overdrive
Artinger Custom Guitars
Fender Twin
Fulltone OCD Obsessive Compulsive Drive

Track 51 Drive, fuzz, distortion
Artinger Custom Guitars
Fender Twin
    a) Clean
    b) Drive - Fulltone OCD Obsessive Compulsive Drive
    c) Fuzz - Vintage Electro Harmonix Big Muff Pi
    d) Distortion - Fulltone Plimsoul

Track 52 Reverb

Artinger Custom Guitars

Fender Twin

    a) Spring

    b) Plate

    c) Chamber

    d) Large chamber ambience

Track 53 Delay

Artinger Custom Guitars

Fender Twin

T.C. Electronic Nova Repeater

Track 54 Multiple Delays

Artinger Custom Guitars

Fender Twin

T.C. Electronic Nova Repeater

Track 55 Looping

Artinger Custom Guitars

Fender Twin

Track 56 Tremolo

Artinger Custom Guitars

Fender Twin

Boss TR2 Tremolo

Track 57 Vibrato

Artinger Custom Guitars

Fender Twin

Track 58 Chorus

Artinger Custom Guitars

Fender Twin

    a) Pigtronix Quantum Time Modulator

    b) MXR Micro Chorus

Track 59 Whammy pedal

Artinger Custom Guitars

Fender Twin

Boss Super Shifter

Track 60 Octave pedal

Artinger Custom Guitars

Fender Twin

Pitch Fork Electro-Harmonix Polyphonic Pitch Shift

Track 61 Harmonizer

Artinger Custom Guitars

Fender Twin

Pitch Fork Electro-Harmonix Polyphonic Pitch Shift

Track 62 Flanger

Artinger Custom Guitars

Fender Twin

Line 6 Liqua Flange

Track 63 Phaser

Artinger Custom Guitars

Fender Twin

MXR Phase 90 Phaser

Track 64 Wah wah

Artinger Custom Guitars

Fender Twin

Dunlop Cry Baby Classic Wah

Track 65 Volume swell

Artinger Custom Guitars

Fender Twin

Ernie Ball VP Jr. Classic Volume Pedal

Track 66 Common combinations

Artinger Custom Guitars

Fender Twin

    a) T.C. Electronic Nova Repeater + Pigtronix Quantum Time Modulator

    b) T.C. Electronic Nova Repeater + Distortion - Fulltone Plimsoul

    c) Distortion - Fulltone Plimsoul + Dunlop Cry Baby Classic Wah

    d) T.C. Electronic Nova Repeater + MXR Phase 90 Phaser

    e) OverDrive - Fulltone OCD Obsessive Compulsive Drive + Pigtronix Quantum Time Modulator

Track 67 Unique Combinations

Artinger Custom Guitars

Fender Twin

    a) T.C. Electronic Nova Repeater (Double delay setting) + Pigtronix Quantum Time Modulator

    b) MXR Phase 90 Phaser + OverDrive - Fulltone OCD Obsessive Compulsive Drive

    c) Boss TR2 Tremolo + Distortion - Fulltone Plimsoul + T.C. Electronic Nova Repeater

    d) Line 6 Liqua Flange + Distortion - Fulltone Plimsoul

Track 68 Ring modulator

Artinger Custom Guitars

Fender Twin

Track 69 Amp modeling

Artinger Custom Guitars

Amplitude

Track 70 Overdub A

Bayard Guitar and Artinger Custom Guitars

Fender Twin

Track 71 Mic distance

Artinger Custom Guitars

Fender Twin

    a) One foot away

    b) Five feet away

Track 72 Extreme effects

    a) Eventide H3000 + Phaser + Delay + Reverb

    b) Distorted signal in parallel to dry signal + 2 delays

    c) Random delay + Unfiltered Audio

Track 73 Unorthodox stringing

Traveler Guitar Sonic L-22

Track 74 Etude 1: Delicate

Bayard Guitars

Track 75 Etude 2: Walk to Run

Artinger Custom Guitars

Fender Hot Rod Deluxe

Track 76 Etude 3: Rain

Fender Stratocaster 1999 American Standard

Fender Twin

Track 77 Etude 4: Shadow Dance

Artinger Custom Guitars

Fender Hot Rod Deluxe

Pigtronix Class A Boost

Track 78 Etude 5: Please Stay

Bayard Guitars

Track 79 Etude 6: Time In

Artinger Custom Guitars

Fender Twin

Pigtronix Philosopher's Rock Compressor

Track 80 Etude 7: Bird Songs

Artinger Custom Guitars

Fender Twin

    a) Boss TR2 Tremolo

    b) Pigtronix Quantum Time Modulator

    c) T.C. Electronic ND-1 Nova Delay

Track 81 Etude 8: Jazz Hard

Artinger Custom Guitars

Fender Twin

Distortion - Fulltone Plimsoul

Track 82 Etude 9: Ocean Lights

Artinger Custom Guitars

Fender Twin

    a) Line 6 Liqua Flange

    b) Fulltone OCD Obsessive Compulsive Drive

Track 83 Etude 10: Exit

Artinger Custom Guitars

Fender Twin

    a) Dunlop Cry Baby Classic Wah

    b) Pitch Fork Electro-Harmonix Polyphonic Pitch Shift

About the Authors

Jake Hertzog

Jake Hertzog is a critically acclaimed guitarist, composer, and educator whose career to-date has spanned nine albums as bandleader across jazz, rock, and classical new music styles. He has toured throughout the U.S., Europe, Latin America, the Middle East, and India and performed and recorded with a diverse cadre of artists, including Randy Brecker, Ivan Neville, Mike Clarke, Blondie Chaplin, Anton Fig, Corey Glover, Barry Altschul, Dave Leibman, Ingrid Jensen, and many others.

Jake's projects have included his jazz group, the Jake Hertzog Trio, the band the Young Presidents, who have been featured on VH1 and MTV, and most recently, *Well Lit Shadow* (2016), a classical suite for solo electric guitar celebrating themes and images in particle physics.

As an educator, he is on faculty at the University of Arkansas, Fayetteville. Jake has been an artist-in-residence and guest clinician in colleges and conservatories in the U.S., Europe, Latin America, and India. He created the instructional series "Hey Jazz Guy" for *Guitar Player* magazine and contributed over 30 articles to the publication.

Jake is a grand-prize winner of the Montreux Jazz Guitar Competition, holds a performance degree from Berklee College of Music, and earned a master's degree from the Manhattan School of Music in New York.

Artist Website: **www.jakehertzog.com**
Educational Website: **www.heyjazzguy.com**

Ueli Dörig

Ueli Dörig is a multi-instrumentalist, music educator, and performing artist. He grew up in Rorschach, Switzerland where he got a bachelor degree in education. After some years of teaching in public school and serving as a Swiss Army musician, he went on to study at the Berklee College of Music in Boston, where he graduated with distinction in both performance and jazz composition. Since 2007, he has lived in Canada's Capital region (Ottawa/Gatineau).

Ueli Dörig is the author of the following educational music books:

- *Saxophone Sound Effects* (Berklee Press, 2012)
- *Trumpet Sound Effects* (Berklee Press, 2014; co-authored with Craig Pedersen)
- *Flute Sound Effects* (Berklee Press, 2016)
- *Saxophone University* (Hal Leonard, 2017)
- *Guitar Sound Effects* (Hal Leonard, 2018)

For more information, visit **www.uelidoerig.com**.

Get Better at Guitar

...with these Great Guitar Instruction Books from Hal Leonard!

101 GUITAR TIPS
INCLUDES TAB

STUFF ALL THE PROS KNOW AND USE
by Adam St. James

This book contains invaluable guidance on everything from scales and music theory to truss rod adjustments, proper recording studio set-ups, and much more. The book also features snippets of advice from some of the most celebrated guitarists and producers in the music business, including B.B. King, Steve Vai, Joe Satriani, Warren Haynes, Laurence Juber, Pete Anderson, Tom Dowd and others, culled from the author's hundreds of interviews.

00695737 Book/Online Audio $16.99

AMAZING PHRASING
INCLUDES TAB

50 WAYS TO IMPROVE YOUR IMPROVISATIONAL SKILLS
by Tom Kolb

This book/audio pack explores all the main components necessary for crafting well-balanced rhythmic and melodic phrases. It also explains how these phrases are put together to form cohesive solos. Many styles are covered – rock, blues, jazz, fusion, country, Latin, funk and more – and all of the concepts are backed up with musical examples. The companion audio contains 89 demos for listening, and most tracks feature full-band backing.

00695583 Book/Online Audio $19.99

BLUES YOU CAN USE – 2ND EDITION

by John Ganapes

This comprehensive source for learning blues guitar is designed to develop both your lead and rhythm playing. Includes: 21 complete solos • blues chords, progressions and riffs • turnarounds • movable scales and soloing techniques • string bending • utilizing the entire fingerboard • and more. This second edition now includes audio and video access online!

00142420 Book/Online Media................................$19.99

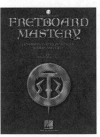

FRETBOARD MASTERY
INCLUDES TAB

by Troy Stetina

Untangle the mysterious regions of the guitar fretboard and unlock your potential. *Fretboard Mastery* familiarizes you with all the shapes you need to know by applying them in real musical examples, thereby reinforcing and reaffirming your newfound knowledge. The result is a much higher level of comprehension and retention.

00695331 Book/Online Audio $19.99

FRETBOARD ROADMAPS – 2ND EDITION

ESSENTIAL GUITAR PATTERNS THAT ALL THE PROS KNOW AND USE
by Fred Sokolow

The updated edition of this bestseller features more songs, updated lessons, and a full audio CD! Learn to play lead and rhythm anywhere on the fretboard, in any key; play a variety of lead guitar styles; play chords and progressions anywhere on the fretboard; expand your chord vocabulary; and learn to think musically – the way the pros do.

00695941 Book/CD Pack...$14.95

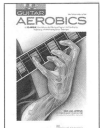

GUITAR AEROBICS
INCLUDES TAB

A 52-WEEK, ONE-LICK-PER-DAY WORKOUT PROGRAM FOR DEVELOPING, IMPROVING & MAINTAINING GUITAR TECHNIQUE
by Troy Nelson

From the former editor of *Guitar One* magazine, here is a daily dose of vitamins to keep your chops fine tuned! Musical styles include rock, blues, jazz, metal, country, and funk. Techniques taught include alternate picking, arpeggios, sweep picking, string skipping, legato, string bending, and rhythm guitar. These exercises will increase speed, and improve dexterity and pick- and fret-hand accuracy. The accompanying audio includes all 365 workout licks plus play-along grooves in every style at eight different metronome settings.

00695946 Book/Online Audio $19.99

GUITAR CLUES
INCLUDES TAB

OPERATION PENTATONIC
by Greg Koch

Join renowned guitar master Greg Koch as he clues you in to a wide variety of fun and valuable pentatonic scale applications. Whether you're new to improvising or have been doing it for a while, this book/CD pack will provide loads of delicious licks and tricks that you can use right away, from volume swells and chicken pickin' to intervallic and chordal ideas. The CD includes 65 demo and play-along tracks.

00695827 Book/CD Pack...$19.95

INTRODUCTION TO GUITAR TONE & EFFECTS

by David M. Brewster

This book/CD pack teaches the basics of guitar tones and effects, with audio examples on CD. Readers will learn about: overdrive, distortion and fuzz • using equalizers • modulation effects • reverb and delay • multi-effect processors • and more.

00695766 Book/CD Pack...$14.99

PICTURE CHORD ENCYCLOPEDIA

This comprehensive guitar chord resource for all playing styles and levels features five voicings of 44 chord qualities for all twelve keys – 2,640 chords in all! For each, there is a clearly illustrated chord frame, as well as *an actual photo* of the chord being played! Includes info on basic fingering principles, open chords and barre chords, partial chords and broken-set forms, and more.

00695224..$19.95

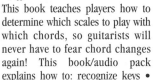

SCALE CHORD RELATIONSHIPS
INCLUDES TAB

by Michael Mueller & Jeff Schroedl

This book teaches players how to determine which scales to play with which chords, so guitarists will never have to fear chord changes again! This book/audio pack explains how to: recognize keys • analyze chord progressions • use the modes • play over nondiatonic harmony • use harmonic and melodic minor scales • use symmetrical scales such as chromatic, whole-tone and diminished scales • incorporate exotic scales such as Hungarian major and Gypsy minor • and much more!

00695563 Book/Online Audio $14.99

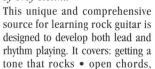

SPEED MECHANICS FOR LEAD GUITAR
INCLUDES TAB

Take your playing to the stratosphere with the most advanced lead book by this proven heavy metal author. *Speed Mechanics* is the ultimate technique book for developing the kind of speed and precision in today's explosive playing styles. Learn the fastest ways to achieve speed and control, secrets to make your practice time really count, and how to open your ears and make your musical ideas more solid and tangible. Packed with over 200 vicious exercises including Troy's scorching version of "Flight of the Bumblebee." Music and examples demonstrated on the accompanying online audio.

00699323 Book/Online Audio $19.99

TOTAL ROCK GUITAR
INCLUDES TAB

A COMPLETE GUIDE TO LEARNING ROCK GUITAR
by Troy Stetina

This unique and comprehensive source for learning rock guitar is designed to develop both lead and rhythm playing. It covers: getting a tone that rocks • open chords, power chords and barre chords • riffs, scales and licks • string bending, strumming, palm muting, harmonics and alternate picking • all rock styles • and much more. The examples are in standard notation with chord grids and tab, and the audio includes full-band backing for all 22 songs.

00695246 Book/Online Audio $19.99

DELUXE GUITAR PLAY-ALONG

AUDIO ACCESS INCLUDED

The Deluxe Guitar Play-Along series will help you play songs faster than ever before! Accurate, easy-to-read guitar tab and professional, customizable audio for 15 songs. The interactive, online audio interface includes tempo/pitch control, looping, buttons to turn instruments on or off, and guitar tab with follow-along marker. The price of each book includes access to audio tracks online using the unique code inside. The tracks can also be downloaded and played offline. Now including PLAYBACK+, a multi-functional audio player that allows you to slow down audio, change pitch, set loop points, and pan left or right – available exclusively from Hal Leonard.

1. TOP ROCK HITS
Basket Case • Black Hole Sun • Come As You Are • Do I Wanna Know? • Gold on the Ceiling • Heaven • How You Remind Me • Kryptonite • No One Knows • Plush • The Pretender • Seven Nation Army • Smooth • Under the Bridge • Yellow Ledbetter.
00244758 Book/Online Audio $19.99

2. REALLY EASY SONGS
All the Small Things • Brain Stew • Californication • Free Fallin' • Helter Skelter • Hey Joe • Highway to Hell • Hurt (Quiet) • I Love Rock 'N Roll • Island in the Sun • Knockin' on Heaven's Door • La Bamba • Oh, Pretty Woman • Should I Stay or Should I Go • Smells Like Teen Spirit.
00244877 Book/Online Audio $19.99

3. ACOUSTIC SONGS
All Apologies • Banana Pancakes • Crash Into Me • Good Riddance (Time of Your Life) • Hallelujah • Hey There Delilah • Ho Hey • I Will Wait • I'm Yours • Iris • More Than Words • No Such Thing • Photograph • What I Got • Wonderwall.
00244709 Book/Online Audio $19.99

4. THE BEATLES
All My Loving • And I Love Her • Back in the U.S.S.R. • Don't Let Me Down • Get Back • A Hard Day's Night • Here Comes the Sun • I Will • In My Life • Let It Be • Michelle • Paperback Writer • Revolution • While My Guitar Gently Weeps • Yesterday.
00244968 Book/Online Audio $19.99

5. BLUES STANDARDS
Baby, What You Want Me to Do • Crosscut Saw • Double Trouble • Every Day I Have the Blues • Going Down • I'm Tore Down • I'm Your Hoochie Coochie Man • If You Love Me Like You Say • Just Your Fool • Killing Floor • Let Me Love You Baby • Messin' with the Kid • Pride and Joy • (They Call It) Stormy Monday (Stormy Monday Blues) • Sweet Home Chicago.
00245090 Book/Online Audio $19.99

6. RED HOT CHILI PEPPERS
The Adventures of Rain Dance Maggie • Breaking the Girl • Can't Stop • Dani California • Dark Necessities • Give It Away • My Friends • Otherside • Road Trippin' • Scar Tissue • Snow (Hey Oh) • Suck My Kiss • Tell Me Baby • Under the Bridge • The Zephyr Song.
00245089 Book/Online Audio $19.99

7. CLASSIC ROCK
Baba O'Riley • Born to Be Wild • Comfortably Numb • Dream On • Fortunate Son • Heartbreaker • Hotel California • Jet Airliner • More Than a Feeling • Old Time Rock & Roll • Rhiannon • Runnin' Down a Dream • Start Me Up • Sultans of Swing • Sweet Home Alabama.
00248381 Book/Online Audio $19.99

8. OZZY OSBOURNE
Bark at the Moon • Close My Eyes Forever • Crazy Train • Dreamer • Goodbye to Romance • I Don't Know • I Don't Wanna Stop • Mama, I'm Coming Home • Miracle Man • Mr. Crowley • No More Tears • Over the Mountain • Perry Mason • Rock 'N Roll Rebel • Shot in the Dark.
00248413 Book/Online Audio $19.99

9. ED SHEERAN
The A Team • All of the Stars • Castle on the Hill • Don't • Drunk • Galway Girl • Give Me Love • How Would You Feel (Paean) • I See Fire • Lego House • Make It Rain • Perfect • Photograph • Shape of You • Thinking Out Loud.
00248439 Book/Online Audio $19.99

Prices, contents, and availability subject to change without notice.

HAL•LEONARD®
www.halleonard.com